Samuel Miller Hageman

**The Princeton Poets**

Samuel Miller Hageman

**The Princeton Poets**

ISBN/EAN: 9783337165154

Printed in Europe, USA, Canada, Australia, Japan

Cover: Foto ©Thomas Meinert / pixelio.de

More available books at **www.hansebooks.com**

# Princeton Poets,

COMPILED BY

## S. MILLER HAGEMAN.

PUBLISHED AT PRINCETON, N. J.

PRINTED ON THE UNIVERSITY PRESS.

WILLIAM S. SHARP,
Trenton, N. J.

1879.

TO

THE MEMORY

OF

# JOSEPH HENRY;

## THE POET OF SCIENCE.

———————

For he hath caused to be written on the water, and
the wind, and every whither, the
autograph of sound.

# PREFACE.

I have gathered up on this old ground these literary relics which I have found about it, in memory of notable men and women who have derived their signal education at Princeton, and who must ever belong most to her by intellectual birthright. Such memorials of distinguished merit have had hitherto but a rude and casual keeping, like names cut carelessly on dark old forest trees, and read only in some stray gleam across them. It is time, now that long death hath dealt hardly with many of them, that they should be redeemed once more into each other's company in these choice affections of their gentliest hours.

S. MILLER HAGEMAN.

Princeton, May 8th, 1879.

# BLOOD-ROYAL.

### I.

O fair art thou Princeton, by river and tower !
Thy wide-sounding bell, and thy dark-ivied bower :
O brave are thy temples with book and with throng !
But to woman, fair woman, thy fame doth belong.

### II.

There is not a Palace of Knowledge on earth
That vies with the genius of blood-royal birth ;
After all we have done when our life-dust is laid,
We are but the men that our mothers have made.

### III.

Thy glory, O Princeton, thy glory we sing,
As thy fame o'er the world spreads her lore-laden wing ;
But fairer for us as we crown her again,
Stands woman, fair woman, the mother of men.

# CONTENTS.

## HUMOROUS POETRY.

CHARLES GODFREY LELAND,

(CLASS OF "          .")

Author of " Meister Karl Sketch Book," "Sunshine from Thought,"
" Heine," " Pidgin English," " Hans Breitman's Ballads,"
" Poems," " Gypsies," &c., &c.

---

# THE RETURN OF THE GODS.

---

Greece so thoroughly wrought out its conception of the beautiful
human animal as to make an idol of it, and in order to glorify it on
earth they made a divinity of it in heaven.—*The Philosophy of Art.*
(*Taine.*)

LIKE one who looks over a city when day is beginning
    to break,
I look o'er the millioned-homed age where we live in
    the dusk of the dawn ;—
Seeing the sunlight on steeples, or edging the turrets and
    towers,
While the streets and the low-lying houses are grey in
    the gloaming or gloom.
Light in the eye of the thinker, light on the brow of
    the wise,
Dimmering shade in the spirit of him who is hopeless
    and low.

Venus, the life of the lovely,—soul of the exquisite
charm !
Thou hast done penance for Ages, as we thy poor chil-
dren have done.
Short was the carnival season, in the gay godland of
Greece,
Few were the guests at the banquet, brief was the life
of the flowers,
Long was the Lent which came after, bitter the wailing
and woe ;—
But the trial was good for the mourners, it humbled the
cruel and proud,
It raised up the humble and fallen, gave spirit and
strength to the poor,
And is freeing from slavery, woman, the slave of all
ages gone by.


Enough of the sack-cloth and ashes, enough of the
penance and pain,
Enough of deep woe for the Many, and feverish joy
for the Few ;
Joy that defeats its own wishes, and struggles in hard,
narrow rounds,
Ignoring the truth that great pleasure demands the
great concourse of All.

O mother of rapture and beauty—thou too hast done
    penance in grief,
Thou didst rise from the Ocean in glory red glowing to
    kiss the warm sun!
Short were the luscious embraces,—cold blew the wind
    from the north,
Thou fell'st in sad tears from Heaven, and on earth
    wert a torrent of tears.


Now in comfort with justice and beauty and freedom
    for woman and man,
Thou wilt rise in a rosier glory, and light every soul
    with a ray.
For when man shall have learned that the spirit of sin
    is but trespass and pain,
Trespass and pain on his fellow, or idle neglect of his
    own,
And that pleasure which injures none other and wounds
    ·  not the spirit of truth,
Has nothing in common with evil, and touches none
    other but self,
Then thou wilt be with us, sweet mother, and charm
    every soul with thy smile,
Raising to Art all our labor—and love be the life of the
    World.

Mars, the magnificent master of warfare with foes to
    the gods,
Brilliant and bold and unbending, thou too wilt rise on
    with the rest,
For the progress of Man is the progress of gods in the
    infinite scale.
He who lifts up the spear to do battle lifts also the
    pennon and steel,
And though the point shine in the sunlight or gleam in
    the glory of war,
Far over the head of the knight it must wait till the
    wood has been raised ;
While man is deep buried in valleys his gods live on
    mountains above,
When he reaches the silvery summits,—they dwell in
    the gold of the sky.


No more the Messiah of murder will Mars be the terror
    of man,
No longer the dread of the lovely, the bravo exulting
    in blood.
For in the great fight of the Future our foes will be
    mightier far
Than men of mere sinew, and muscle, those foes which
    lie silent around ;

The rugged rock-giants denying the room for existence
   to all,
The awful deep Dragon of Ocean still keeping in secret
   its plains,
And the solemn blue space yet unconquered which parts
   us from numberless stars,
And the Fire-Land which burns in our centre, these
   foes still await thee, O Mars!


For the doctor who drives out diseases or shortens the
   power of death,
And the teacher who quickens the spirit and conquers
   the darkness of crime,
The poet, who blesses with beauty the soul that was
   gloomy and grey,
The builder, the chemist, the workman, are warriors
   each in their way ;
For what were the Jotunds and Titans o'erwhelmed by
   the gods of the Past,
But the forces of fire and of mountains, the giants we
   are fighting to-day.
Fighting more bravely than ever, fighting with better
   success :
O Mars, thou wert in the first battle—in the victory be
   by our side!

I know that the swift-footed Hermes will soon be be-
    lovèd again,
For already man finds with strange rapture he holds
    more than Mercury's power,
More than the might which was fabled to be that of
    Hermes of old
When he touches the telegraph deftly and talks over
    oceans afar,
As we go faster in motion, faster in thought and in
    speech,
Quicker in means of conveying and shortening the path
    of ideas,
Life will be lengthened while growing, for thought is
    the measure of life,
He who speaks or does most in a little is Mercury's son
    and himself.


And with Labor and Love and with conquest and speed
    all the rest will be won,
With Vulcan and Venus and Ares and Hermes fast
    darting afar,
For Apollo with Muses and Graces, the exquisite chil-
    dren of art—
And the sense of the lovely in Nature as shown in a
    myriad gods,

All these are just hovering around us awaiting a place
    in our hearts,
Not as wearied-out forms of a worship which faded
    long ages ago.
But as the fresh life of all worship, renewed in Mars'
    faith in himself,
The man who has risen to Greatness was never yet
    wanting in gods.


Do your hearts enter into my meaning, ye thinkers who
    list to my song?
Do you feel that we come to religion in quitting the
    vulgar and mean?
And that Man when he lives in the glory of conquest
    and knows he is great
Soon learns that the power of crushing the Time-worn
    means this,—to be free.
Freedom with power creative, greatness with beauty
    and love,
Was, is and shall be forever the God-like in spirit and
    truth.
And be it in smoke upon Sinai, in temples and statues
    in Greece,
Or walking by Galilee's waters, the noble is ever a god,
Grander than Plato or Hegel, greater than Bacon or
    Compte.

Is faith in a noble endeavor, the power to rise to the
    New :
And the scorn of the ancient Egyptian, of Hermes, for
    those who but live
For idle self-will and dull pleasure,—the million who
    nothing create
In the downward-borne elements whirling away from the
    centre of God,—
In the first of the wonderful chapter long written and
    yet to be writ,
Which told, and will tell, how the dawning drove dark-
    ness away from the world,
And how the small sneer of the Devil was lost in God's
    infinite smile.


This is the coming of Zeus,—of Jove, the imperial
    lord !
And of Juno, his wife and his sister, the greatest are ever
    akin,—
That man shall find out he is noble, this knowing he
    finds out a god,
And the glory of God will be with him when dignity
    blesses his life ;
Esculapius teaches this lesson.—The purest of blood are
    most free

In strains, without taint of disorder the nearest come
　　ever more near.
The souls which live Jove-like in calmness, progress in
　　perfecting their type:
What Satan and folly have bidden will rise in the ages
　　to come.


How shall we see the immortals, and when shall we
　　know they are come?
In Greece we behold them in statues,—unmoving im-
　　mortals in stone:
Closed in a book in Judea,—frozen and centred in
　　One,
Blooming again into Many, which flowed from the
　　mythical Three,
And burst into wide-flashing rainbows of legend and
　　color and song.
When the wonderful age mediæval threw pictures all
　　over the world,
Not in statues, or books, or in pictures, or churches, or
　　legends, or song,
Will ye see the great gods of your worship whose foot-
　　steps are sounding afar.

Ah, no;—in yourselves will ye see them when Venus
 shall favor your love,
And man, fitly mated with woman, believes that his
 love is divine:
When Passion shall elevate Woman to something so
 holy and grand,
That she the ideal enraptured shall ne'er be a check
 upon man ;
Then the children they bear will be holy, and Beauty
 shall make them her own,
And Man in the eyes of his neighbor will gaze on the
 reflex divine.
Of the God he inclines to in spirit—or trace in each
 feature and limb,
The lines which the body inherits from souls that are
 noble and true.


Would thou could'st feel in deep earnest how beautiful
 God will be then,
When we see him as Jove or Apollo in men who inspire
 us with love,
As Jambres and Venus the holy in women, who know
 not the mean,
And feel not the influence cruel, of hardness and self-
 love and scorn ;

Would thou could'st once know how real the presence
    of God will become,
How earnest, and ever more earnest, thy faith when thy-
    self shall be great,
And from the true worship of others thou'lt learn what
    is holy in them,
And rise to the infinite fountain of glory which flows
    in us all.


But when shall we see the Immortals? Believe me
    whenever we will,
They are near us, around us, within us, awaiting our
    wish and our word,
More than thy dreams ever pictured, more than thy
    heart ever dreamed,
Will pour increasing abundance on him who has free-
    dom and faith ;
Freedom from meanness and harshness, faith in the
    Godhood within—
The ore lies before us in mountains, we've power to
    change it to gold ;—
Be to thyself what thou lovest, and others will be unto
    thee
What thou wilt. When in God thou believest, near
    God thou wilt certainly be.

# GHOST-LAND.

---

## FAIRY MYTHOLOGY.

---

All over doth this outer earth
    An inner earth enfold ;
And sounds may reach us of its mirth
    Over its pales of gold.
There spirits dwell—unwedded all
    From the shapes and shades they wore ;
Though oft their silent footsteps fall
    By the hearth they loved before.
We mark them not, nor hear the sound
They make in circling all around ;
    Their bidding sweet and voiceless prayer
    Float without echo in the air.
Yet, often in unworldly places,
    Soft sorrow's twilight vales,
We meet them with uncovered faces,
    Outside their golden pales ;

Yet, dim as they must ever be,
Like ships far off, and out at sea,
   With the sun upon their sails.

And he who once hath raised his eyes
   Oh, soul of love, to thee !
From ·that day forth, beneath the skies,
   No other sight can see.

# WOMAN'S WILL.

Con la muger y el dinero,
No te burles, companero.

MANY a charm is round thee,
Many a spell hath bound thee,
Though awhile I'll give thee leave to range.
Soon, thy wild flight over,
Soon, no more a lover,
Back thou'lt fly and never dare to change.
If thou wilt, go, flutter
Here and there to utter
Burning words to all, with wanton will.
But—thou can'st not leave me,
No—nor once deceive me,
And in chains I hold thee captive still.

To some love enchanting,
Every favor granting,
Go and sigh—I bid thee—'tis in vain!
For no woman clever
Lost a lover ever,
When she willed to, hold him in her chain.

She who's sure of winning,
When the game's beginning
Throws away of course a stake or two ;
But when higher aiming,
Bent on bolder gaming,
Back they come, and then she holds them true.

B

# MINE OWN.

And O the longing burning eyes!
  And O the gleaming hair!
Which waves around me night and day,
  O'er chamber hall and stair.


And O the step half dreamt, half heard,
  And O the laughter low;
And memories of merriment
  Which faded long ago.


And some do call me Wantonness,
  And some do call me Wine:—
O, they might call me what they would
  If thou wert only mine!


And some do call me Life sweetheart,
  And some do call me Death:
And he to whom the two are one
  Hath won my heart and faith.

She twined her white arms round his neck,
The tears fell down like rain ;
"And if I live or if I die
We'll never part again."

# EYES.

Eternal eyes of wonder,
  How gloriously they rolled ;
Like two black storm-lakes under
  An autumn-forest of gold.

# THE LORÉ-LAY.

[*German of Heine.*]

I know not what sorrow is o'er me,
    What spell is upon my heart,
But a tale of old times is before me,
    A legend that will not depart.


Night falls as I linger dreaming,
    And calmly flows the Rhine;
The peaks of the hills are gleaming
    In the golden sunset-shine.


A wondrous lovely maiden
    Sits high in glory there;
Her robe with gems is laden,
    And she combs her golden hair.


And she spreads out the golden treasures,
    Still singing in harmony;
And the song has a mystical measure
    And a wonderful melody.

The boatman when once she has bound him,
　Is lost in a wild sad love;
He sees not the rocks around him,
　He sees but the beauty above.


I believe that the billow springing
　The boat and the sailor drown;—
And all that, with her magical singing,
　The Loré-lay has done.

# TRANSLATIONS.

[*German of Heine.*]

Wait, oh wait, impatient sailor,
  Fast enough my footsteps stir;
From two maidens I am parting—
  From Europa and from her.


Lovely cradle of my sorrow!
  Lovely tomb of peace to me!
Lovely town, we part to-morrow,
  And farewell,—I cry to thee.


Sacred home,—you'll see me never—
  Nevermore where she has strayed;
Home, farewell,—we part forever,
  Where I first beheld the maid.

# SUNSET.

Die glübend rothe sonne steigt.

[*German of Heine.*]

The sun in crimson.glory falls
Down to the broad up-quivering
Gray and silvery ocean-world.
Airy figures, warm in rosy light,
Wave-like roll after;—while eastward rising
From autumn-like darkening veils of vapor,
With sorrowful death-pale features,
Breaks the silent moon.
Like sparks of light behind her
Cloud distant, glimmer the planets.


Once there shone in Heaven,
    Nobly united,
Luna, the goddess, and Sol, the god,
And the bright-thronging stars in light
    Swam round them,
Their little and innocent children.
But evil tongues came whispering quarrels,

And they parted in anger,
The mighty, light-giving spouses.—


Now in the daytime, in loveliest light,
The sun-god walks yonder in glory—
All for his lordliness.
Ever prayed to and sung by many,
By haughty, heartless, prosperous mortals—
But still by night
In Heaven wanders Luna,
The wretched mother,
With all her orphaned starry children,
And she shines in silent sorrow,
And soft-loving maidens and gentle poets
Offer her songs, and their sorrows.

## "IN THE HOLLOW OF HIS HAND."

The great and restless ocean rolls
  Resistless on the sand,
Yet every wave is measured in
  The hollow of His hand.


Each separate drop that teems with life,
  Each billow far from land,
Or angry crested-breaker, knows
  The hollow of His hand.


Help us, O Lord, for faith grows dim ;
  We do not understand ;
Our seas of woe sure *must* o'erflow
  The hollow of Thy hand.


Teach us that all are measured there,
  A sounding deep and grand ;
There are no depths of grief *without*
  The hollow of Thy hand.

Each throb of woe, each weary pain
  Of head, or heart, or hand,
The long-drawn hours of sickness—all
  Are measured in Thy hand.

These waves can never rise too high,
  For Thou wilt help us stand.
Dear Lord, we cast our burdens in
  The hollow of Thy hand.

# TRANSLATIONS.

[*From Heine.*]

They loved so well,—yet neither
  Would have the other know;
They met as foes—yet either
  For love would life forego.

They parted, and met never,
  Save in the dear dream-land.—
They died, and still as ever,
  *They do not understand.*

[*From Heine.*]

A noble fir tree lonely stands
  On northern height so cold;
He sleeps,—all covered deep with snow,
  And decked with icy fold.

His dreams are of a lovely palm
  Far in the summer land,
That drear and lone all sadly stands
  By rock and burning sand.

*[From Heine.]*

My songs have all been blighted,—
  How could they live with strife?
Thou hast poured a burning poison
  On the blossom of my life.


My songs have all been poisoned,—
  How could they but depart?
With so many, many serpents
  And thee within my heart.

---

## THE LILY AND THE MOONBEAM.

*[From the German.]*

The moon hangs in the dusky night,
  All silver-clear above,
And pours the splendor of her light
  On streamlet and on grove.


From sweetest dream she rouses up
  The lily, tenderly,
And opes its little snowy cup
  To set the fragrance free.

The fairest moonbeam ever seen
　　Glides in that open breast,
And nestles 'neath the tender screen
　　With thousand kisses pressed.


Then closes tight the beauteous flower,
　　And holds the wooer fast,
Who, resting in the lily bower,
　　Finds peace and joy at last.


Next morning when the shepherdess,
　　With merry, childish zest,
The lily plucks in eagerness,
　　And clasps it to her breast;


Then, when the chalice opened lies,
　　She feels a wondrous pain,—
An unknown longing quickly flies
　　Through every glowing vein.


Now wandering through the leafy bower
　　She sighs, the livelong night:
Say? did the moonbeam in the flower
　　Work out its spell aright?

# SILENTIO.

Slowly climb the moon-fringed mountains, like a stair-
way to the sky,
Slowly each white cloud ascending seems a soul that
passed on high;
Summits billowing after summits grander and still
grander grow,
Till they break in awful silence on a glittering strand
of snow.

Silent cataract of summits, stiffened on thy frozen
verge,
Thundering down in deafening silence to thy adamantine surge;
Motionless, yet grandly moving, seems thy avalanche
of stone,
Silenceniatus be thou everlasting on thy solitary throne.

At thy base the swirling river chatters idly to the clod,
At thy brow thy head is lifted through the veil to talk
with God,

Prophet-like with mantle folded round thy dread and
    spectral form,
Far below thee screams the eagle, far below thee raves
    the storm.


Greatness lies insphered in silence, littleness to sound is
    stirred,
All the grandest things in nature never have been seen
    or heard ;
Proving down by printless logic all the science of the
    school,
Silence is the law of being, sound the breaking of the
    rule.


Wind was flourishing its trumpets, but th' embattled
    air is still,
Streams were roaring down the gorges they have thrided
    to a rill,
Thunder charioted the Heavens, but its rumbling wheels
    have sped,
Man was talking to his fellow, but the man grew dumb
    and dead.

Far into the past I wandered, paused within its mellow
    clime,
Where the Lethean years were crossing at the Jabbok-
    ford of time.
Felt the boundaries of being sink around me into
    space,
Listened—but could hear no echo, looked—but saw nor
    form nor face.

Noiselessly the round creation slowly rose into its
    place,
Like the moon at night ascending up the star-sloped
    stairs of space;
To its walls there came no workman, to its towers no
    touch of hand,
Without sound like some great palm-tree spreading
    over sea and land.

What is history? half-blown silence lifting leaf by leaf
    its bud,
Be it read by book or battle, be it traced by drops of
    blood:
Providence the perfect poem of a God whose life is love
Set on earth to seeming discord, set to music far above.

Silence on the palid face-cloth, silence on the snowy
  grave,
Silence on the sleeping city—silence far below the
  wave,—
Silence as of music slumbering on her harp within the
  deep :—
Sound is but the dream of silence, silence talking in its
  sleep.


Once my heated soul was looking from the window of
  its hope,
And before it lay life's landscape, and the sun was on
  the slope ;
Far I leaned into the future, from the old into the new,
But my breath hath blurred the glass, and stained the
  vision from my view.


Hear a broken voice within thee struggling with the
  perfect will,
Hush it in the strong submission of thy spirit and " be
  still : "
Stillness in which thou shalt hear the falling of a lifted
  rod,
Stillness in which thou shalt hear the full-orbed whisper
  of a God.

Somewhere on this shipwrecked planet, in the mist of
    years to be,
In the silence, in the shadow, waits a loving heart for
    thee;
Somewhere!  Where art thou, O spectre of illimitable
    space?
Silent sphere without a shadow, silent sphere without a
    place.


Break, O break this bitter silence, speak unto me once
    again!
Tell me, shall I e'er behold thee? tell me, do I wait in
    vain?
O my mother! O my mother! ship beneaped on foreign
    shore;—
Answerless the air around me, answerless forevermore.


I shall slumber, but it recks not where my lonely grave
    be made,
Whether you and I together in a kindred ground are
    laid:
I shall slumber, but it recks not who shall touch me in
    the gloom:
Twins that sleep within the cradle are not twins within
    the tomb.

All things yet shall work together, and so working orb
　　in one,
As the sun takes back his sunbeams, when the dial-day
　　is done.
All things yet shall ripen roundly, and unite and shape
　　and climb
Into truth's great golden unit in the long result of time.


Wisdom ripens unto silence as she grows more truly
　　wise,
And she wears a mellow sadness in her heart and in
　　her eyes:
Wisdom ripens unto silence, and the lesson she doth
　　teach,
Is that life is more than language, and that thought is
　　more than speech.


What is truth?　Thy jeweled finger points like light
　　with swerveless trend,
From the Orient of knowledge down the path that hath
　　no end:
What is truth?　Religion ponders, science strains her
　　listening ears—
Through the fallow of the future break the seeds of
　　silent years.

Faith is but an idle canvas flapping on an idle mast,
If it be not found within thee as the work of life at
last;
Dotaged faith is but a fancy—he who waits that dream
is lost,
And his creed a cursed millstone, and his God a chilly
ghost.


Very like the soul is sleeping soundly underneath the
sod—
Very like the soul is walking softly overhead with
God—
Likelihood alone is certain. Who shall speak while
God is dumb?
Credent doubt is but the shadow of the larger faith to
come.


O thou strong and sacred silence, self-contained in self-
control;
O thou palliating silence, Sabbath art thou of the soul:
Like snow upon my virtues lie like dust upon my
faults,
Silent when the world dethrones me, silent when the
world exalts.

Tamper not with idle rumor lest the truth appear to lie,
Carve thy life to hilted silence, wrong shall fall on it
and die:
Tamper not with accusation, harvest not what thou hast
heard,
Christ stood in the Court of Pilate, but he answered
not a word.


Silence is the voice of spirit, silence is the voice of God,
Since He said "Go preach My gospel" he hath never
spoken word:
Many a power since then hath perished, many a charm
hath lost its spell,
But that ever-silent spirit still on earth is ruling well.


Spoken to but never speaking, dimly felt but never
found.
Silence after every prayer, silence after every sound,
Can it be we pour our spirits out into a godless air?
Can, oh can it be that death shall drift us over to
despair?

Dips the white sail of my spirit down the trending sea
of death,—
Silent sea without a ripple, save the ripple of a breath,
Moving out for pass or shipwreck without signal, gun,
or light,
To the phantom-pilot rounding on the misty reef of
night.


Turn me on my fevered pillow, for the night is turning
too,
I will bolster up my courage, I will see what death
can do—
Death whose spectre stalks so coldly. What is death?
(we do thee wrong),
But life stopping in its singing to take breath for endless song.


At the centre of creation lies a spot of summer rest,
Where the silent spirit broodeth like a white dove on
its nest:
Round it runs the deep horizon in its golden quiet
curled,
Round it at the wheel of motion spins the fashion of
the world.

Ever after mortal effort, ever after mortal pains,
Something to which light is shadow, something unex-
pressed remains.
Ever after human question, ever after human quest,
Something farther than the farthest, something better
than the best.


God shall keep the sparkless secret of the silence in His
heart,
Through the crescent years of knowledge, through the
golden days of art:
Silent heart, whose birthless beatings throb so softly in
their place,
That God cannot hear himself in all the continent of
space.

AARON BURR,

(Class of "1772.")

# MY MESSAGE–BIRD.

[*From the Round Table.*]

Wing, wing thy flight, my faithful message bird
To her I may not seek—sh'll welcome thee;
Take to her heart this tale which thou hast heard
Fall from her lips, so oft alone with me.


Fly, fly, nor stop to rest thy aching wing,
'T'will weary not as tires my heart the while;
Breathe in her ear that she may bid thee bring
Back to my waiting lips a kiss or smile.


Haste, haste, sweet messenger, take wing and start,
And in thy absence think how I must burn;   .
But stay,—drop in her breast this throbbing heart,
And bring back hers, or nevermore return.

# KNIGHTS TEMPLAR.

The Templar-Knights are laid to rest—
In sign of what they loved the best,
Their hands are crossed upon their breast.


They march no more to Palestine,
Nor quaff her purple, sacred wine,
Nor watch her glowing suns decline.


To guard their Lord's beloved fane
No more they cross the surging main,
Nor redden with their blood the plain.


We love to turn the storied page
And read the battles they did wage
In distant mediæval age.


To turn to lady's bower they left,—
Perchance by some wild crag, or cleft
In mountain side by lightning reft.

To see in some ancestral hall
Stern armor hanging on the wall—
And light of romance over all.


To hear the harper's notes resound,—
And while the vassals gather round,
To list of that far battle-ground.


But are there left no Knights? A few
Unswerving hearts with purpose true
Might right all wrongs, all chains undo.


Is not Christ's tomb to us as dear
As though we kept with lance and spear
Its portals through the changing year?


Hath past the golden age of faith,
When, with her name on failing breath,
Men showed they loved her to the death?


No,—Faith still lives, and Christ, we see,
Must servèd be far differently—
We fight for all humanity.

In caring for all souls oppressed,
And leading them to peace and rest,
We follow still our Lord's behest.


The Templar once might guard His tomb—
We guide the pilgrim through life's gloom
Towards the Heavens whence He shall come.


We throw our lance for all mankind—
And he indeed can be but blind
Who doth not still true knighthood find.

# JAIRUS' DAUGHTER.

The little maid had died, believing that the Christ would
    come,
Bringing with His presence healing to her home.
And now the Master enters, turns to those who weep,
And speaks these words for all the ages,—"Death is but
    a sleep."


And so from death's dark slumber, and with no surprise,
Her eyes she opened, hearing Christ say softly, "Maid,
    arise."
For this was not a stranger—she had listened for His
    feet
In quiet expectation, till her heart had ceased to beat.


And we had dear ones who believed the Master's care
Was such, that ev'n in death they did not know despair.
In faith and hope sublime they closed their patient
    eyes :—
His foot was on the threshold—He would say, " Arise."

# NIGHTS IN JUNE.

[*From the French of Victor Hugo.*]

In summer when the day hath fled, clad in verdure and
in flowers
Sends the plain full many a mile away, the fragrance of
her bowers.
With eyes half-closed and every sense by lightest murmur stirred,
Transparent is our slumber like the sleep of any bird.


Then the stars are brighter, purer, and the shadows
softer lie,
And the dawning pale and tender seems to wander
'neath the sky,
Watching all the vague half-lights that tint Heaven's
distant dome—
Waiting long and patiently—waiting for her hour to
come.

# THE PILGRIM OF ST. JUST.

Charles V. retired to the Monastery of St. Just, in Estramadura, in the north of Spain, and there ended his days.

[*From the German of Count von Platen.*]

Night falls—the storm-winds ceaseless roar—
Ye Spanish friars open to me your door.


Let me rest here till the matin-bell
Shall call to prayer, and the anthem's swell.


Prepare for me, with pious grace,
A brother's dress—a burial-place.


Grudge not a cell to one of royal line;
The land of half this world was mine.


This head I offer for the tonsure's shears
Hath worn a crown through weary years.

Imperial ermine graced the form
That seeks a shelter from the storm.


I see Death beckon—hear him call—
And, like my kingdom, into ruin fall.

# THE ROSE AND THE GRAVE.

[*From the French of Victor Hugo.*]

The grave said to the pale blush-rose,
"What dost thou, fairest flower that grows,
With mist and dew that water thee?"
The rose looked up and made reply,
"What doest thou with those who lie
Within thy vaults, all hopelessly?"


The rose said, "Sombre grave, I know
That all these tears of grief must go
To make my perfume strong and sweet."
The tomb said, "Holy souls I take,
And of them angel-spirits make,
To rise one day with wingèd feet."

D

# MADRIGAL.

[*From the Italian of Ménage to Madame de La Fayette.*]

Ah, vainly Phillis, wouldst thou ask
How long shall last my love for thee!
To answer were too hard a task :—
Who knows when death shall set me free?

# "DRINK TO ME ONLY WITH THINE EYES."

Drink to me only with thine eyes,
  O lovely damozel!
No goblet quaffed beneath the skies,
  Boasts wine I love so well.


Thy bare, thy beautiful white arm,
  Thy bosom's fall and rise,
Thy voice that hath such power to charm,
  But O thine eyes, thine eyes!


Those sweet inebriating eyes,
  Cupbearers to the soul,
Work in me stronger spell than lies,
  Within the dizzy bowl.


O deep exhilarating thrill
  That warms me to the heart,
Go, reveler, haste fresh cups to fill,
  This draught will not depart.

Drink to me only with thine eyes,
O lovely damozel!
And let me feel my spirit rise,
Upon the working spell.

# THEN AND NOW.

---

## A SUMMER IDYL.

---

All through the slowly-gliding afternoon,
Under the wide, blue wonder of the June,
That like the motherlook in some fair face,
Broods over it with gentle warmth and grace,
Stirred only here and there by passing feet,
Drowses and dreams the pleasant village street

Silent and cool like a cathedral aisle,—
And rich mosaics wrought of sunbeams' smile,
And shadows' tender gloom pave the long way;
Now and then a wood-robin's ringing lay
Floats through the silence, as if echoes fell
Across still waters from a distant bell.

Out beyond where the elms and lindens meet,
In dainty clasp above the village street,

As if fair faces through an open door
Looked, and fair hands waved to another shore,
The crimson glory of the sunset streams,
Wooing one from this lotus-land of dreams.


Toward the red west the winding pathway goes
Thro' velvet grasses, a white line it grows,
And all the infinite of Summer sky,
And earth's untarnished green about it lie.
O perfect hour! can there be anywhere
Bowers where faded leaves and flowers are?


All the wide air is fragrant, fresh and still,
Yet tremulous with the deep throb and thrill
Of holy presence, as if God had stood
Here, and pronounced this new creation "good,"
As in that first fair Summer-time, whose birth
The morning stars greeted with song to earth.


Brimful with evening's dusky red and gold,
Like stately urns that ruddy liquids hold,
On the hill stands the row of regal pines;
Up and down where a tangle of lush vines
Falls from it, lies the path; shallow and wide
Below the brook goes with its languid glide,

Flushed rosily, like a child's face in sleep;
Under the arched bridge pools lie clear and deep
In the brown shadows; beyond, smooth and slow
Between the dipping trees the waters flow
With white glints; by the old mill wheel at rest
The path goes on into the glowing west.


Long ago, long ago in another June,—
Young hearts and the young summer-time in tune—
On this same path beyond the shady town
Two walked, a youth and maiden, up and down
Together by the brook; t'was morning then;
With little flashing leaps the waters ran


Chased by light breezes; how the clear air rang
With the gay songs red-breasted robins sang:
How the dews sparkled, and the ambient blue
And gold of June with glory girt those two;
Their life was in its buoyant, glowing June,
Morning so far, so far from afternoon.


And lightly down the winding path they walked,
The youth and maiden, and as lightly talked;
Laughter and banter, jest and repartee,
With the brook's chatter blended gleefully,—

Yet the brook had its low, sweet undertone
That the vine bending to it heard alone.


And those two walking in the summer weather,
By the bright waters down the path together,
Talking so lightly, did not each heart hear
Undertones of the other heart anear?
Perchance,—and yet, and yet the story old,
So many Junes have heard remained untold.


O memory, how often thou art but
Another word for a life-long regret!
To a thing of the past silently grew
That blithe June morning, and between those two
Pitiless seas came, and no more together
They roamed, the youth and maid, in Summer
        weather.


One walking down the old path now alone
In the rich wine-light, hears like a low moan
The whispering brook, and watching dreamily
The day's fair dying, thinks Ah me! Ah me!
That other June, how long, how long ago!—
T'was morning then, and it is evening now.

# STILLED VOICES.

We hearken for them in the dreary silence
That falls with the long shadows of the years;
Woo them with tones from anguished spirits starting,
Tremulous, passionate, with hopeless tears.


We sit apart in lonely, shady places,
Listening, listening in the twilight gloom;
Sometimes soft footfalls glide in with the shadows,
And the stilled voices float across the room.


They are but echoes stirred in memory's chamber,
As if one strayed thro' festive halls, where glee
And lights and music in white day had vanished,
And dreamed he heard the past night's revery.


We walk in crowded ways, and song and laughter
Sweep by with passion undertoned or pain;
Yet there's a missing part in this world-chorus
We ever wait and listen for in vain.

We tread the green home-paths worn and familiar,
  And rest in wonted bowers; but they have grown
Wintry and wan, palled in a stirless silence,
  With the familiar voices from them flown.


There is a blue sea stretching far, relentless,
  And mocking, with its deep, defiant roar,
Hearts that on this side wearily are yearning
  To hear the voices on the other shore.


There is a blue sky calmly doming over
  Green waves of earth which buried treasures keep;
Lips that spoke pet names once the grasses cover,
  Desolate ones left here above them weep.


Clasped hands are lifted to that far-off azure,
  Eyes pleading dumbly, cries that are a prayer;
Beyond it is the fair celestial city,
  And voices that we miss are singing there.


But cry and gaze part not those pearly portals,
  And the far jasper walls no strains float o'er.
O God! this longing in the dreary silence
  For the dear voices stilled forevermore.

# PICTURES.

## I.

Stately and tall and glimmering white,
Like a fair phantom trancing the sight,
Rises a mansion out of the night.


Fluttering visions of fair face and form,
Soft gala strains, lights mellow and warm,
Float on the dark, stream out on the storm,


Out on the bent form, on the wet hair
Of one who shivers shelterless there,
Round him, within him, night and despair.


## II.

Midsummer noon, a road white with heat;
Under the sunbeams' pitiless beat
One walking there with faltering feet.

High garden walls the dusty way bound,
Over them thro' the still noon's profound,
To the tired traveller come the cool sound

Of crystal fountains plashing their showers;
Delicate wafts from banks of fair flowers;
Low insects' hum from green depths of bowers.

Outside the walls no light shadow-play,
Spice-breathing blossoms, cool fountain spray,
Straight, blinding white goes on the highway.

### III.

Touched with the calm of evening skies,
Flushed as if sea-shells' opaline dyes
Gleamed through its depths, a fair harbor lies.

White sails like gulls glide over its floor,
Prows gaily turn to homes on the shore,
Hearth-lights leap forth from window and door.

Very far out from harbor and home
Night closes down, with wild storm and gloom,
Round a ship driving on to its doom.

Over the surge no signal-lights flare;
No sky-rifts show the star-angels there;
No hushing " Peace, be still," thrills the air.

## IV.

With shine and blue from life's morning skies,
Rippled and laughed in hair and in eyes,
Dreaming child-dreams, a little child lies

Dainty and warm in love's soft embrace,
Glorified with the sweet, tender grace
Shed from a mother's ineffable face.

Outside the clasp of white arms of love,
Unguided, weary little feet rove.
It has no rest—the innocent dove.

O, orphaned ones on whose guileless eyes
Earth's touch of sorrow so early lies,
Angels yearn to you out of the skies!

O lonely ones of earth, desolate,
Standing unsheltered, outside the gate,
Festival halls and joys for you wait!

O, ye who faint in hot ways, beside
Cool fountains where the " still waters " glide
Through the " green pastures," you shall abide.


O, hapless ships that far out at sea,
Through the wild black night drift helplessly,
Safe in port yet at last you shall be.

# NOTHING ELSE TO-NIGHT.

Softest radiance, saintliest splendor
   Fills the autumn-night;
Sky and stream and hill and meadow,
   Teem with silver light.

Gazing out I know that beauty's
   Spell has touched this spot,
But my heart holds other visions
   And it sees these not.

Over miles of hill and forest
   Sees the moonlight lave,
In a wide, wan solitude,
   An unshadowed grave.   .

Strange upon the marble's whiteness,
   In the moon's cold gleam,
Looks to-night the carving of that
   Dear familiar name.

\*    \*    \*    \*    \*    \*    \*    \*

O my sister !   O my sister !
    If I might to-night,
Through the shimmer of the moonbeams,
    Catch the angel-light


Of your face one flitting moment,
    Such a joy 'twould be !
I should know by it you were not
    Quite, quite lost to me.


If, from out the throbbing silence,
    Like a faint, far chime,
I might hear you whisper, "Darling,"
    As in the old time !


But there is no voice,—no vision,
    Only white moonlight
Wrapping shroud-like grave and marble,
    Nothing else to night.

# A SABBATH DREAM.

O holy beauty of the holy hours!
A sense of color fused from grass and flowers,
Of splendor in the sunshine's lavish gold,
Of sound thro' silver harps of silence rolled,
Is here like a far-off dream memory,
Or waft of recollected fragrancy.

But all the long day eyes enchanted turn,
And all the long day hearts with longing yearn
To the blue sky-deeps where nor stain nor scar
Of earthly cloud and earthly shadow are.
And through the long days' hush those sweet words ring:
" Not having spot or wrinkle or such thing."

  &ast;  &ast;  &ast;  &ast;  &ast;  &ast;  &ast;  &ast;

Beautiful skies! tired eyes rest in your blue,
And weary human spirits yearn to you.
So near and yet so very far away,
You smile back to us this long Sabbath day.
O if so fair this side of Heaven we see,
What must the glory of the other be?

E

FITZ HUGH LUDLOW,

(CLASS OF "    .")

# TO THE HOME OF ALL LIVING.

Garden of the quiet dead,
 Seed-ground of Eternity,
Many a weary heart and head
 Longs for silence and for thee.
Here shall sorrow's hand no more
 Sweep the soul's discordant strings ;
And the lyre that oft before
 Thrilled to love's young carolings,
Voiceless lies from morn till even ;
But it shall be woke in Heaven.


Island art thou of the Blest,
 In life's ever-heaving sea ;
Here earth's weary ones may rest
 From the billows' mockery.
Rage ye winds that vex the sky,
 Chilling summer into death ;

But where those sweet sleepers lie
  Hush your voices to a breath :
Kiss the roses till they yield
  Perfume from the stilly field.


Heaven's entrance-way thou art
  From beggar's hut and chair of state ;
The throbbings of the dying heart
  Are only knockings at thy gate.
Other homes may scorn to yield
  Shelter from the bitter rain,
At thy doors O burial-field,
  Pilgrim never knocked in vain.
On thy breast we yet may fall,
Earth, thou mother of us all !


Lulled to sleep in thine embrace
  Many a weary babe shall lie,
And the chief whose visored face
  Blanched not at the battle-cry.
Here no more the bride shall dream
  Of the rose less fair than she,
And olive-shaded academe
  Shall fade from Plato's memory.
O mysterious place of rest
Take thy children to thy breast.

# NIAGARA.

Niagara! I am not one who seeks
   To lift his voice above thine awful hymn;
Mine be it to keep silence while God speaks,
   Nor with my praise to make his glory dim.


Yet unto thee, shape of the stony brow,
   Standing forever in thine unshared place,
The human soul within me yearneth now,
   -And I would lay my head beside thy face.


King from dim ages of God set apart
   To bear the weight of a tremendous crown,
And feel the robes that wrap thy lonely heart,
   Deaden its pulses as their folds flow down.


What wondrous years are written on the scroll
   Of thy imperial dread inheritance;
Man shall not read until its lines unroll
   In the great hand that set thy stony trance.

Perchance, thy moveless, adamantine look,
  For its long watch o'er the abyss was bent,
Ere the thick gates of primal darkness shook,
  And light broke in upon thy battlement.


And when that sudden glory lit thy crown,
  And God lent thee a rainbow from His throne,
E'en through thy stony breast flashed there not
    down
Somewhat of His joy also made thy own.


Who knoweth but he gave thee to rejoice
  Till man's hymn sounded through the time to be,
And when our choral coming hushed thy voice,
  Still left thee something of humanity.


Still seemest thou a priest, still the veil streams
  Before thy reverent eyes, and hides thy sight:—
And thine is as the face of one who dreams
  Of a great glory now no more his right.


Soon shall I pass away; the mighty psalm
  Of thine o'er-shadowing waters shall be heard
In memory only, but thy speechless calm
  Hath lessons for me more than many a word.

Teaching the glory of the soul that bears
  Great floods, a veil between Him and the sun,
And, standing in the might of Patience, dares
  To bide His finishing who hath begun.

## A LA DAME A VOILE NOIRE.

As night the rosy-bosomed hills unfolding
  Softens their tracery in his weird embrace,
So more ethereal grew the matchless moulding
  Of thy pure, earnest, spiritual face,
      Most pensive maid,
      Beneath the shade
Of that strange veil of melancholy lace.


Art thou an abbess gliding from the chancel
  Where Eloisa poured her soul and prayed,
Unshrouded and revivified to cancel
  Some debt of Christian charity unpaid
      In years agone
      When the midnight tone
Of death's cold angel made thy heart afraid?


Or art thou but a type of death's own essence?
  Unearthly beauty whose dark borderings
Turn men's hearts chill with horror at his presence,

And make them slaves who timely shall be kings.
 But if a Heavenly gale
 Lifts up the veil,
Straightway they're ravished with death's inner things.


Perchance thou art a beautiful temptation,
 Some mystic bodiment of deadly sin,
Like her, who in the veil of consecration,
 Mixed with the orizons of Capuchin,
  Him nightly wooing,
  To his undoing,
Till to his lost soul Satan entered in.


Thou art too beautiful—I'll look no longer,
 For be thou woman, phantasy or sprite,
A spell is coming on me that is stronger
 Than silence in the watches of the night,
  For good or evil,
  From saint or devil,
I dare not lift my eyes to read aright.

# ODE TO NIGHT.

O lovely mother night!
Thy breath is cool,
 And on my fevered brow
 I feel it now
Like angel's hand dipped in Bethesdan pool.


O lovely mother night!
Like tired sheep
 Within thy star-watched fold,
 The young and old,
The strong and weary shall lie down to sleep.


The bride whose loved-culled wreath
Withered anon,
 More than the jasmine fair,
 Shall slumber where
The warrior lies dead with his harness on.

And O how sweet and still
That rest shall be ;—
    Beneath the shadowy pall
    That broods o'er all,
Expanding into immortality.

PHILLIP PENDLETON COOKE,

(Class of "1834.")

Author of "Froissart Ballads," Poems, &c., &c.

---

## FLORENCE VANE.

---

I loved thee long and dearly,
   Florence Vane;
My life's bright dream and early
   Hath come again.
I renew in my fond vision
   My heart's dear pain,
My hopes and thy derision,
   Florence Vane.


The ruin old and hoary,
   The ruin old,
Where thou didst hark my story
   At even told.
That spot—the hues Elysian
   Of sky and plain—
I cherish in my vision,
   Florence Vane.

Thou wast lovelier than the roses
　　In their prime;
Thy voice excelled the closes
　　Of sweetest rhyme;
Thy heart was like a river
　　Without a main :
Would I had loved thee never,
　　Florence Vane!


But fairest, coldest, wonder,
　　Thy glorious clay,
Lieth the green sod under.
　　Alas, the day!
And it boots not to remember
　　Thy disdain—
To quicken love's pale ember,
　　Florence Vane.


The lilies of the valley
　　By young graves weep,
The daisies love to dally
　　Where maidens sleep;
May their bloom in beauty vying
　　Never wane,
Where thine earthly part is lying,
　　Florence Vane.

## MANY A YEAR AGO.

Many and many a time together,
    Many a year ago,
By this stream in summer weather,
    Two, wandered slow.
But from me too soon she parted,
    Fore'er below—
Beautiful and broken-hearted,
    Many a year ago.


Fairer than the flowers I brought her
    Many a year ago,
Lies that face upon the water
    That haunts me so.
Fairer now than I can fashion
    In Heaven, I know,
She, who loved me in her passion,
    Many a year ago.


Moon and wood and sliding river,
    Many a year ago,

With her sigh still seem to shiver,
  For her young woe.
Little dreamed I then, fair maiden,
  I loved thee so,
Whom I left to sorrow laden,
  Many a year ago.

J. ADDISON ALEXANDER,

(Class of "1826.")

## THE DOOMED MAN.

There is a time we know not when,·
A point, we know not where,
That marks the destiny of men
To glory or despair.


There is a line by us unseen,
That crosses every path,
The hidden boundary between
God's patience and His wrath.


To pass that limit is to die,
To die as if by stealth;
It does not quench the beaming eye,
Or pale the glow of health.


The conscience may be still at ease,
The spirits light and gay;

That which is pleasing still may please,
And care be thrust away.


But on that forehead God has set
Indelibly a mark,
Unseen by man, for man as yet
Is blind and in the dark.


And yet the doomed man's path below,
Like Eden's may have bloomed;
He did not, does not, will not know,
Or feel that he is doomed.


He knows, he feels that all is well,
And every fear is calmed;
He lives, he dies, he wakes in hell,
Not only doomed, but damned.


O, where is this mysterious bourn,
By which our path is crossed;
Beyond which, God himself hath sworn,
That he who goes is lost?

How far may we go on in sin
  How long will God forbear
Where does hope end, and where begin
  The confines of despair?


An answer from the skies is sent:—
  " Ye that from God depart,
While it is called *to-day* repent,
  And harden not your heart."

F

# TO THE RHINE.

Lines composed on re-crossing the Rhine at Coblentry.

I hail thee as an ancient friend,
  And as I cross thy line,
My democratic knee I bend
  To greet thee, royal Rhine.

The day and hour when last we met
  Come o'er me like a dream;
As then I saw, I see thee yet,
  Unchanging, changing stream.

The rush of waters o'er thy bed
  Distracts my labouring brain;
Forever dying, never dead,
  Buried, yet born again.

What is the secret of thy life
  What holds thy channel fast?
Amids't the elemental strife
  The earthquake and the blast.

Why is it that the swollen tide
  Which ever northward sweeps,
So warily on either side
  Its well worn station keeps?


Why dost thou not, old Rhine, at length
  Burst thy ignoble chains,
And mustering all thy mighty strength,
  Submerge th' adjacent plains?


Thou art a king among the streams,
  Thou river deep and broad :
In regal pomp thy surface gleams
  To man, but not to God.


Thy full deep current bold and proud,
  In His almighty view,
Is but the sprinkling of a cloud,
  A drop of morning dew.


Though thou shoulds't empty every rill,
  And drain the neighboring land,
Thy giant waters could not fill
  The hollow of His hand.

The same almighty hand that drives
　　Thy current to the sea,
Can well control it when it strives
　· And struggles to be free.


And if at times that hand grows slack,
　　And lets thee do thy worst,
He brings thee still at pleasure back,
　　And rules thee as at first.


So, when I bend my stubborn knee
　　To greet thee, royal Rhine,
I render homage not to thee,
　　But to thy Lord, and mine.

# SEA BIRDS, WILD SEA BIRDS!

Sea Birds, wild sea birds!
Wreckers of the white-capped wave,
Wheeling on the winds that rave
Off by stormy cliff and cave,
　　Sea Birds, wild sea birds.
　　　Swooping, dipping,
　　　Round the shipping
Cradled on the billow's grave.
　　Out upon yon treeless ocean,
　　In its calm and its commotion,
　　Mocking back its restless motion,
　　Sea Birds, wild sea birds.


Sea Birds, wild sea birds!
Where the petrel-lightning leaps,
Where the wolf-wave never sleeps,
Where the eagle-tempest sweeps,
　　Sea Birds, wild sea birds!

Wildly whirling
Through the swirling
Surges of the yeasty deep.
By yon bifurcated gleaming,
See!   A ship is sinking, steaming,
And upon its mast-tops screaming,
Sea Birds, wild sea birds.


Sea Birds, wild sea birds!
Hooting at the fowler's dart,
Laughing at the angler's art,
Scoffing compass, sail and chart,
Sea Birds, wild sea birds.
On the pillow
Of the billow,
Rocked like child on mother's heart.
Nor within the forest nested,
Far from them upon the crested
Wave, sleeps bird so softly breasted,
Sea Birds, wild sea birds.


Sea Birds, wild sea birds!
So like you with wingèd haste,
Wheels my soul upon her waste,

Swept by sorrow and effaced :
    Sea Birds, wild Sea Birds !
    And like shadows
    Eldorado's
Are the phantoms it has chased.
    Still that wild, bright sea I covet,
    With the clear blue sky above it,
    Land of sea birds, O I love it,
    Sea Birds, wild sea birds.

# THE LAST BANQUET OF ANTONY AND CLEOPATRA.

Once more, O lady, let our mirth's wild clangor
　Ring to the keystone of the midnight sky,
Then sinking, rouse a thrill of jealous anger
　　In dusty hearts that deep in old tombs lie.
To-morrow, sweet, may lay us down beside them,
　To-night is ours—crown it with wine and song,—
Teach its dark moments in thy locks to hide them,
　Bind, witch, these hours to linger with thee long.

\*　　\*　　\*　　\*　　\*　　\*　　\*

What wild and wondrous note was that went pealing
　Up to the keystone of the midnight sky?
Echo? What dim and ivied shapes go reeling
　On through the gate where Cæsar cometh nigh?
Antonius! thy country's gods forsake thee—
　Not e'en the god of Mirth will longer dwell
Where strength and virtue are not. Sleep! nor
　　wake thee
　　From Cleopatra's arms,—Dishonor's hell.

# THE BLOOMING OF THE CEREUS.

There came a low tap at my chamber door,
  When o'er Night's back the mighty moon-shield hung;
Before Fear's chilly hand stole wholly o'er
  My heart, the door I swung.


Lo! there stood maiden Iris, morning-eyed;
  How 'frighted Fear then spread his dull bat-wing
Rainbow at night! What word of Jove, I cried,
  Dost from Olympus bring?


Arise! Arise! and haste thee, Caroline!
  A breath just floated thro' my slumbers dumb,
That said: I hold my court, a kingdomed queen,
  To-night, my hour is come.


The Cereus blooms. "Quick! by our Lady's grace,"
  Cried Iris, bringing net and tying sash;
Then each an arm in arm we interlace,
  And through the darkness dash.

Far shone her father's house.   Around 'twas sweet
　　As if a sky-borne censer swung down there;
Roused neighbors thronged like courtiers fain to greet
　　A kingdom's longed-for heir.


Three hours we watched her growing ever fair,
　　And radiating joy with every breath—
And then we watched her fading, fading—Dear!
　　It seemed a great queen's death.


O Land! that blossomed late in earth's long night,
　　Thy first bloom drew the wondring nations' gaze;
Shall they, too, see thee, ere the coming light
　　Fade as a flower decays?

# A FANTASY.

[*From "Scribner's."*]

If I awoke some morn,
And down the stairs descending, all forlorn
Of wonted faces found the world below,—
No mother's smile, no kiss, no baby's crow,
No sister taking up the thread, half-spun,
Of last night's talk (some talks are never done:)


Outside the door
If then I wended, seeking soft Lenore
Or welcome, stately-sweet of Lady Clare
Or stayed my step at gracious Anna's stair
Or sought gay Lili for a tilt of words
Keen and inspiriting as tourney swords;


And here and there,
For whisper of the wise, smile of the fair,
For all gay courtesies, lightsome pleasantries,

For the dark splendor of some gorgeous eyes
For even thee, soul comrade, if a bare,
Blank, very vacancy should on me stare.


     If then should speak
Some right authentic angel : They you seek
All like a dream have vanished : but a dream
In truth they ever were ; they did but seem,
Phantasmas were they, figments, fantasies,
Projections of thy own thought, only these.


     Ah me, alas !
If all this grammarye should come to pass
I think I should believe him ;—should believe :—
Nor would his disenchantment deeply grieve,
Nor greatly startle, nor bewilder me
Soul-comrade, save, 'twere also told—of thee.

# THE PHYSICAL BASIS.

## ACCORDING TO SHELLEY.

When the lamp is shattered,
The light in the dust lies dead;
When the cloud is scattered,
The rainbow's glory is fled;
When the lute is broken,
Sweet sounds are remembered not;
When the lips have spoken,
Loved accents are soon forgot.

## A PROTEST.

When the lamp is shattered,
The light re-ascends its throne;
When the cloud is scattered,
The parted rays make one;
When the lute is broken,
The heart-strings echo yet;
When—some lips have spoken,
Ah! would that we could forget!

# WITHOUT AND WITHIN.

Cold as the breath of Azrael,
Without the storm-wind rose and fell,
And roared and raved, and drove and hurled
Dead branch upon dead branch, and whirled
To shreds the dead year's shroud, laid o'er
Her softly, all the night before,
By pious care of snow elves mild.
O shrieking wind! so fierce and wild,
Canst thou be he God made last Spring,
His angel, odor-balms to bring
O'er earth and sea?   Wilt burst the door?
God keep the old!   God help the poor!


Within a round white altar burned
With vestal heat, that soared and spurned
The cold from farthest alcove deep,
Where Art and Wisdom lay asleep;

It carried Summer up on high,
Where violet, rose, and primrose lie,
In glowing panes that warm the light,
And fling it bright on marble white—
Dark floor, and desk, and earnest brow,
Grown pale for love of Thought, I trow.


Around that altar seemed to sigh
A far, faint breath of Araby,
Mild odors from Malayan strands;
While from a row of pictured lands,
I take, down moonlit balconies,
Clear, graceful founts, that never freeze,
But, dimpling in glad sun-heat play,
From Christmas-Tide to Easter-Day.
Circled by Moorish columns' grace,
I hear no more the snow-wind's race,
I see no white and whirling drift,
Only those calm cathedrals lift
Their glory in blue Summer air,
Here—costume quaint; there—fancy rare.
So Art and I together there
Clasped loving hands while outside rolled
The din of fiends, Chaos and Cold!
Ah! but they fly, they faint, expire
Before these angels, Art and Fire!

# THE CONVENT SISTERS.

An incident related in Montalembert's "Monks of the West."

Night upon the convent shone,
Kissed the towers of august stone,
Down the cloisters deep and wide,
Night and peace went side by side;
Tower and crypt, and arch and wall,
Night and silence wrapt them all.


Bears the chilly midnight air
Breath of incense—note of prayer?
Lauds and incense far uprolled,
Safe the golden vials hold;
Back soft wings of sleep have flown,
Hark! Whence is that hollow moan?
From the lone and patient cell,
Of poor sister Isabel.


Her, the holy mother chideth,
That her grief too long abideth:

Her, the father penance gave,
That her heart too fondly clave
Round a fellow mortal's grave.


Ah ! poor sister Isabel,
If 'tis sin to love too well,
In a world of wrath and scorn,
Better thou had'st ne'er been born !
Work and prayer your grief will calm ;
Meek she tries each holy charm,
Washes all the long stone floor,
Where she walked with Isadore :


Plucks away rank autumn weeds,
Where they sowed glad summer seeds ;
Binds alone for Mary's shrine,
The wreath she always helped her twine ;
Bends above some wayward child
Asking questions, quaint and wild ;
Hard for fitting answer tries,
And thinks how Isadore was wise.


O ! the blank in Lauds and Prime,
Where that voice was wont to chime ;

G

O! the dread hush in Compline,
Where it should come sweetly in!
But in dreams she hears it—hark!
Her soul leaps—waking in the dark.


Quick she springs up—kneels repeating
O'er the song just heard—the fleeting
Spirit so to chain—in vain!
She's gone! She ne'er will come again!
O my love! What bars may fret thee?
What strange pains make thee forget me?
Hear, O Lord! I ask no more,
But light and peace give Isadore!
On the stone she falleth prone,
On the still air spreads her moan.


Clear and low, and sweet and full,
Breaking through her anguish dull,
What is that? Whose are those eyes,
Shining calm, yet eager, wise?
" Understand me, my beloved,"
Spake the vision, " be not moved."


"Already I in great peace dwell,
But I know not, Isabel,

How to enter paradise
Without thee; so love arise :
At thy quickest haste fulfill
All thy task remaining still ;
Then come! For I wait to adore Him,
Till we two can kneel before Him."


When the third chill midnight shone,
The task of Isabel was done.

E. P. T.

# IGIORNI CHE PASSAN.

---

[*From the Italian.   By a Lady.*]

Errante solitario
Fra rupe e fra foresti,
Le pene mie funesti
Qui vergo a racon tar.


Non tremola una foglia :
Il vento non respira
Solo il mio cor sospira
I giorni che passan.


E della valle tacita
In ogni rupe e speco,
Mesto risponde un eco
Ai lagni dell' amor.


Oh, fosse quello il vivido
Accento del mio bene !
Finesti questi pene,
Sarebbero nel cor !

JAMES WADDELL ALEXANDER,

(Class of " 1820.")

# O SACRED HEAD.

O Haupt voll Blut und Wunden.

*[From the German of Gerhardt.]*

O Sacred Head, once wounded !
With grief and shame weighed down,
Now scornfully surrounded
With thorns, thy only crown.
O Sacred Head, what glory,
What bliss, till then was mine!
Yet, though despised and gory,
I joy to call thee mine.


O noblest brow and dearest!
In other days the world
All feared when thou appearedst;
What shame on thee is hurled!

How art thou pale with anguish,
  With sore abuse and scorn!
How doth that visage languish,
  Which once was bright as morn.


The blushes late residing
  Upon that holy cheek;
The roses once abiding
  Upon those lips so meek;—
Alas! they have departed;
  Wan death has rifled all:
For, weak and broken-hearted,
  I see thy body fall.


What thou my Lord hast suffered,
  Was all for sinners' gain:
Mine, mine was the transgression,
  But thine the deadly pain.
Lo! here I fall, my Saviour!
  'Tis I deserve thy face;
Look on me with thy favor,
  Vouchsafe to me thy grace.


Beside thee, Lord, I've taken
  My place; forbid me not;

Hence will I ne'er be shaken,
    Though thou to death be brought.
If pain's last paleness hold thee
    In agony opprest ;
Then, then I will enfold thee
    Within this arm and breast.


The joy can ne'er be spoken
    Above all joys beside,
When in thy body broken,
    I thus with safety hide.
My Lord of life, desiring
    Thy glory now to see,
Beside the cross expiring,
    I'd breathe my soul to thee.


What language shall I borrow
    To thank thee, dearest Friend
For this, thy dying sorrow,
    Thy pity without end !
Oh, make me thine forever,
    And should I fainting be,
Lord, let me never, never
    Outlive my love to thee.

If I, a wretch, should leave thee,
O Jesus, leave not me!
In faith may I receive thee,
When death shall set me free.
When strength and comfort languish,
And I must hence depart,
Release me then from anguish,
By thine own wounded heart.

## THE PORCH AND THE TEMPLE.

I stand in the porch of a temple
 That rises up out of the night :
Its buttress is buried in shadows,
 Its bell-tower is splendored in light.
Though I pass not on earth thro' its portal
 Where the throngs of the ages have trod,
I know by the signs of its splendor
 That its builder and maker is God.

The sun like a dim burning porch-lamp
 Is shining in front of thy door,
The stars are the lights in thy windows
 That wave their red torches before.
And deep down in crystalline caverns
 That the torch of the traveller hath found,
The rainbow in rock lies resplendent
 In the star-studded night of the ground.

The flowers swung in rare perfumed censors
　Are breathing thy fragrance to me,
The birds are all singing a music
　That shall clasp its full zone-chord in thee.
And everything stands for a prophet
　On the hills that are lifted between,
A mark of invisible beauty
　An image of something unseen.


My soul like a shell that is sounding
　In a strange foreign land of the sea,
Sings ever the wonderful echo
　Of the kingdom of heaven in me.
And sometimes a faint solemn murmur
　Rolls up on the spirit within;
The echo of life everlasting,
　The sound of its strange, silent din.


When the red sun bars in splendor
　The curtains that crimson the sky,
Its gate like an angry garnet
　Blinds brightly the earthly eye.
When I shake off the dust from my sandals
　At the sepulchre's open door,
O how with a spotless footstep
　Shall I tread your crystal floor.

O white-towered city of wonder!
O beautiful homes of the blest!
My heart though it throbbeth in slumber
But knocks at thy closed doors for rest.
But my thoughts as they throng on thy portal
Fall down broken-winged in their flight
Ah! only Death's rusty night-key
Shall open the Palace of Light.

# KNITTING FOR THE SOLDIERS.

Here I sit at the same old work,
Knitting and knitting from daylight till dark ;
Thread over and under, and back and through,
Knitting socks for—I don't know who ;—
But in fancy I've seen him and talked with him too.


He is no hero of gentle birth,
He's little in rank, but he's much in worth ;
He's plain of speech, and strong of limb ;
He's rich in heart, but he's poor of kin ;
There are none at home to work for him.


He set his lips with a start and a frown
When he heard that the dear old flag was shot down
From the walls of Fort Sumter, and flinging away
His tools and his apron, stopped, but to say
To his comrades, " I'm going, whoever may stay,"
And was listed and gone by the close of the day.

And whether he watches to-night on the sea,
Or kindles his camp-fire on "lone Tybee,"
By river or mountain, wherever he be,
I know he's the noblest of all that are there,
The promptest to do, and the bravest to dare;
The strongest in trust, and the last in despair.


So here I sit at the same old work,
Knitting socks for the soldiers from daylight till dark,
And whispering low as the thread flies through,
To him who shall wear them,—I don't know who;—
Ah, soldier, fight bravely, be patient, be true,
For some one is knitting and praying for you.

HORACE BINNEY WALLACE,

(Class of "1835.")

# ODE ON THE RHINE'S RETURNING INTO GERMANY FROM FRANCE.

———

Oh sweet is thy current by town and by tower,
The green sunny vale and the dark linden bower;
Thy waves as they dimple smile back on the plain,
And Rhine, ancient river, thou'rt German again!

.

The roses are sweeter, the air is more free,
More blithe is the song of the bird on the tree;
The yoke of the mighty is broken in twain,
And Rhine, dearest river, thou'rt German again!

The land is at peace and breaks forth into song,
The hills, in their echoes, the cadence prolong,
The sons of the forest take up the glad strain,
"Our Rhine, our own river, is German again!"

Thy daughters, sweet river, thy daughters so fair,
With their eyes of dark azure, and soft sunny hair,
Repeat 'mid their dances at eve on the plain,
"Our Rhine, our own river, is German again!"

# THE PRAYER OF THE FALLEN.

God of the bright, unfallen sun
    That stoops to kiss a wretch like me,
In the whole world there now is none
    To whom my soul may come but thee!
Though ruined and unclaimed my birth,
    Though fallen all my prided charms;
If ruined, 'tis but for the earth;
    If fallen, 'tis within thy arms.

God of the fallen, hear my prayer!
    By all the wounds in Christ that bleed,
O do not leave me in despair,
    • O do not pass the lips that plead.
And thus, though shunned of all I be,
    And thus, though fallen low, I lie:
When we are farthest off from thee,—
    Thou never art to us so nigh.

As the struck eagle on the plain
    Transfixed upon the death-cold dart,

Looks up at the blue sky again
　　That but so lately warmed his heart;
So the spent spirit here below
　　Yearns from its dust to one divine;
And O how sweet it is to know
　　That one so lost as I—am Thine!


God! that the passion of my love
　　Should work in me such lethal spell,
As that the noblest gift above
　　Sets Heaven to sink me down to hell.
O that the genius of my youth
　　Should starve for lack of self-control,
And in the banquet-hall of truth
　　Know but the hunger of a soul!


I wonder on this wintry night,
　　When gathered for the evening prayer,
Whether, though I be far from sight,
　　They think of her who once was there?
Strange that I should be counted thus
　　Because I fell in bolder sin,
Since all who walk the world with us
　　Carry a fallen soul within.

H

I sought the love of Nature's heart,
   I came, and called her by her name,
But she too seemed to stand apart
   And put my sinful soul to shame.
I saw the mountains rise on high ;
   Beneath their burnished crowns of snow ;
They rose up glorious,—but I
   Lay fallen at their feet below.


I saw the brook within its bed,
   And on its tide the willow tree ;
But, when it saw my face, it fled
   To hide its picture in the sea.
I spoke to birds that sang near by ;
   I wooed them with my softest tone ;
They spread their wings upon the sky,—
   And I felt fallen and alone.


The vine, though trampled by the storm,
   And dashed upon the careless ground,
May lift again its fallen form,
   And reach, ere night, the top-most round.
The very dust beneath my feet
   May set itself on windy wing,
To stars along the golden street,
   That light the seraphs as they sing.

But I shall never rise again,
    Though many a wing o'er me be spread,
For, far from women and from men,
    I dwell with the unburied dead.
For them the Sabbath bells shall ring,
    And prayer be given, O God, to Thee,
For them the white-robed choir shall sing,
    But not for me, but not for me.


O that my Saviour, as he stood
    Among that group of old, would stand
By me, and bid, with instant word
    Stone-throwing slander drop it hand!·
O could I hark that lovely voice,
    That gently spoke to one before:
Thy sins are all forgiven.   Rejoice,
    O woman—go, and sin no more!


My mother drove me from her door;
    My name was silenced for my sin;
My father bid me come no more;—
    Father in Heaven, O let me in!
I've wandered in the bitter street;
    I've slept where dangers nightly roam;
The frost hath marked my bleeding feet;—
    Father in Heaven, O take me home!

# FROM THE BARK OF AN OLD TREE.

[*From a Lady's Album.   By a Lady.*]

E'en as a traveler perchance,
  Engraves his name upon a tree,
In hope to win a casual glance,
  And woo remembrance still, when he
A distant wanderer may be ;—
  Thus have I claimed this page of thine,
Be it but reckoned worthy thee,
  And I shall proudly own it mine.

# CRI DE PASSION.

[*From the French. By a Lady.*]

N'aimez-vous pas l'orage,
  Avec ses bruits lointains :
Avec l'éclair qui nage,
  Qui flamboie et s'éteint !
N'aimez-vous pas la foudre,
  Et ses roulements sourds,
Qui rappelle le poudre,
  Battant les vieilles tours.

.

N'aimez-vous pas au coeur,
  Cette voix qui bouleverse,
Cette voix du malheur,
  Qui foudroie et—
Eh bien ! ces ouragans,
  Ces tempêtes de l'ame,
Tout pour les coeurs ardents,
  Ce que c'est pour l'oeil la flamme.

## "SHE IS NOT DEAD."

"She is not dead." Why jesting speak,
  Great Healer, to this scorning herd?
Cold as the ashes of her cheek,
  And dead as marble, sounds that word.

Is not the limner-king at work,
  Lighting his shadows on her brow,
And thine own seal the lines that lurk
  About that sleeping damsel now?

Like leopard in his fevered beat,
  Within an iron compass round,
Tired fancy, with returning feet,
  Toils at this empty, mocking sound.

What means it? Not that death to thee
  Is but her entrance back to life;
For all the scattered graves shall be
  Like trophies in a final strife:

Nor that she lives. Death hath no cell
  In darkest dungeon of the sea
Where sleeper since our mother fell
  Sleeps more the sleep of death than she.


The search seems endless. The hot brute
  That chafes within the cage's walls,
Makes each dull foot-mark, worn and mute,
  Note a glance outward as it falls :


So eager fancy eyes the bed ;
  The waiting group; the bated breath ;
That silent, wondering, pitying dread,
  That bends within thy court, O Death :


And more! Oh miracle and shame!
  The dying daughter's restless hands,
And clouding sight, that groping came,
  As questioning where her father stands ;


Till, faltering, and their purpose lost
  By thicker shadows o'er her eye,
Her love's poor, baffled look has cost
  The last and fatal agony.

These answer not!   Nor yet the street,
    Nor yet the shoutings by the sea,
Nor yet the sound of coming feet,
    Nor yet the Savior's mastery.


Christ has all life; but why should one
    Thus brave the tyrant in his den;
Or go' like Esther to the throne,
    And bring her beauty back again?


There stands the question.   What in her
    Forced death that deadly game to miss?
And where the pulses that could stir
    Life in a livid form like this?


Sudden, like daybreak o'er the sea
    In Summer cycle near the Line,
Light flashes, and the mystery
    Ends at a glance in thought divine.


Jairus!—Not gentle like the girl!
    Not powerful like the Incarnate King!
Go hail him! (proud, disdainful churl!)
    Superb enchanter, life to bring!

The man who nursed his bigot zeal,
  The man who prized his haughty line,
Has forced his envied rank to kneel
  For worship at a hated shrine.


There lay Christ's meaning!  When the slaves
  Came seeking their dishonored lord,
Mark the strange faith; 'tis that that saves
  The daughter by our Savior's word.


The man who suffered life to wane,
  And death to torture undenied,
Watching the ravages of pain
  And weakness at his daughter's side,


Has dashed the bigot in his strength,
  And crushed the zealot in his zeal,
And left the suffering girl at length,
  Meek, at the Peasant's feet to kneel.


No paltering now: to the vile dust
  He brings his forehead and his cry.
And thronging prayers and groans are thrust
  Into the ear of sympathy.

Forgot all Jewry ! What their dread,
  And what their shame about his case,
And what their cry, " The maid is dead,"
  To him who tastes his Master's grace ?


Upright before the face of men,
  Humble before the eye of Heaven,
Mark this grand faith, and take it then
  For answer that our Lord has given.


Go, servants, back, nor waste your breath,
  Nor theirs who say, " Thy child is dead ; "
" She is not dead ; " her father's faith
  Stands victor at the maiden's bed.

# "WHAT IS HIS NAME?"

A SONG OF DEGREES.

"—When they shall say to me, What is his name? what shall I say unto them? And God said unto Moses, I shall be what I shall be: and he said, Thus shalt thou say unto the children of Israel, I shall he hath sent me unto you."—*Exodus, III.*, 13, 14.

"I appeared unto Abraham, unto Isaac, and unto Jacob by the name of God Almighty; but by my name Jehovah (He Shall Be) was I not known to them."—*Exodus, VI.*, 3.

O GOD ALMIGHTY, can there be
A grander name than that for thee?
ALMIGHTY GOD! What lordlier king
For fancy on its wildest wing?


The universe an infant lives
Alone by power thy being gives;
Its myriad ages past, to thee,
An instant in eternity.


Yet God, when beams of mercy broke
On Israel under Pharaoh's stroke,

Thou scornedst this proud name to own,
And as JEHOVAH wouldst be known.


Strange title! Riddle dark and deep
The ages in those letters keep:
Puzzle nor men nor angels see;
Yet simplest legend,—"He Shall Be."


Not what thou wast when world on world
In spendthrift splendor was unfurled;
Nor afterward, when life and death
Hung in the balance on Thy breath;


But what "I shall be," such the name
Thou gavest Moses to proclaim;
JEHOVAH! what "He Shall Be" when
The God descends to dwell with men.


Blest legend! long fulfilled; for now,
In sunlight on the Savior's brow,
Gleams the great name of all the three,
EMMANUEL, what I was to be.

# STRONG DELUSION.

## I.

" Down at the bottom of the churchly pile,
Built in by martyrs,
Lies the hoar relic of a mystic Three,
Supporting all the faith,
And watched by tread of sentinels.


Time cannot change it.
It roots itself in piety.
Baptized into our speech ;
Bright with the colors of the easel's work ;
Attune with minstrelsy :
And all alive with ransom,
And with the throes of earnest prayer ;
It seats itself for other flight of years :
Though, like the 'Night' and 'Morning' in the
    Tomb,
It lies, half cut, within the rock,
And, therefore, as much unseen as seen.

And yet a creature of a month or day
Sets him against the centuries;.
Rejects the doctrine,
Brands it all a cheat,
Burns in the candle of his own esteem;
And, given up to strong delusion to believe a lie,
Is fixed as granite,
Though the world's piety eyes him with pity,
And knows the foot below him is but sand."


## II.


So sang the saintliest; but saintlier from the Throne
Shot forth a messenger,
And blazoned on the cope
Of Heaven's high canopy responsive pictures.


As when coal, sharpened in points,
Heats the white light,
And pours its offering on the curtained wall.


There is a street;
And vulgar crowds are hurrying to Calvary.

The scum of Galilee has claimed to be a God!
Think of it!
The Latin world moves on like stars in space;
And the Augustan age,
Crowded with vast events,
Recks not the history.
Clio has turned her back;
And, afterward, when search is made,
The lying monks have to invent a record.
Great Rome, fixed in the zenith of her strength,
Feels Him like dust upon her chariot.
And yet this beggar, fainting on the ground,
Black clots upon His beard,
And mocking tinsel yet upon His arm,
Grasps at the sovereignty of worlds!


He held a court but now in the Prætorium;
His purple—stolen;
His sceptre—
Afterward to bear the sponge that ministered to
    His pitiable feebleness;
His crown—the weeds clutched from the thorny
    Kedron;
His worship—mockery;
His service—oaths and smitings.

Take this hot moment!
When, knowing He must be mad,
They use Him for a soldier's revel;
Or, better, when the moon looks out.upon His pain,
And weary Salem sleeps away her madness.
Where is the strong delusion?
His? mixed up with murderers?
Or theirs, who sent Him to His death,
Calm in that wealth of faith,—
"Give God the praise;
We know that this man is a sinner?"


A ring of priestly bell, and crumbs of bread
Are turned into the flesh of this same peasant!
Some creature doubts it,
And a cry of injured faith swells to the very
    Heaven,
And broad over every land
Comes the deep sigh of faith
Adjudging martyrdom.
Whose is the strong delusion?


A pitcher lifts the water from the spring,
And pours it on the head of infancy,
And a deep life springs forth!

A priest extends his hand,
And pardon follows on the spoken breath!


A worm crawls blindly from the churchly path,
And the whole world, with pity in her eye, calls
    for his torture.


There is no end to lessons.


Another worm sits on the throne, a madman;
Makes life a curse;
Builds law on perjured wickedness;
And saps even laws like that, with hot impatien-
    cies of villany.
And yet for years and years
The world cries out that he is divine:
And bishops lose their sees;
And statesmen put their heads upon the block,
Rather than say that there is no divinity in kings,
Come there what will.


And so of other things,
Mayhap this multiple of God—the honored Trinity.

I

Delusion bows itself with all its might,
And pulls the fane of faith
Upon its buried worshippers.
But whose delusion is it?
Is it the blind Samson?
And all the Lords safe in their might?
And Dagon on its pedestal?
Or is it the shorn victim coming to his strength;
And the crushed captive blessing most,
Just in his saddest hour?

# OUR DEAD,

[*From a Lady's Sketch-Book.*]

Grief cannot win them back,
  And yet with frequent tears
We bring to mind their cherished forms,
  With thoughts of other years ;—
With love, that neither death nor change
Hath power to sever or estrange.


We cannot blot them out
  From memory's written page ;
We cannot count them strangers, but
  Like birds in prison cage,
We beat against the iron bar,
That keeps us from those friends afar.


Oblivion may not hang
  Its curtain o'er their graves ;
There is no water we can sip
  Like Lethe's lulling wave ;

But fond affection's moaning wail
Breaks from us like the Autumn gale.


Ye are not dead to us,
  But as bright stars unseen
We hold that ye are ever near,
  Though death invades between.
Like a thin cloud that veils from sight
The countless spangles of the night.

## AS CHILDREN FOLD THEIR SLEEPY FACES.

As children fold their sleepy faces
  Within the breast that gave them birth,
So do the dead in quiet places
  Turn them to thee, O Mother Earth !

What though the snow shall whiten on us,
  A warmer robe we never knew ;
What though the rain fall oft upon us,
  So fell our mother's tear-drops too.

I go—but not to greet a stranger ;
  To thee our friends for quiet went ;
And in thy lap through calm and danger
  Our little life hath all been spent.

And as we travelling ever nearer
  Touch in the grave God's garment-hem,
Thou art to us, O Earth, the dearer
  For all that thou hast done for them.

On thy firm lips forever closes
　The awful secret kept in thee;
And thy calm face no line discloses
　Of earthly guilt or misery.


For, be thy grave by land or billow,
　To traveller in its midnight-inn,
'Tis but the turning of a pillow
　To cool the fever-flush of sin.


I know not to what worlds beyond thee,
　Those sleeping travellers are bound;
I only know the flowers that frond thee
　Are breathing pity all around.


Banquet of Rest! affection's roses
　Shall drink to thee, O Mother Earth!
In golden wine where love reposes,
　The pledge of an immortal birth.


Against a grave within a garden,
　Rosebuds by night beat out their breath,
Till to God's knock they seemed to harden,—
　'Twas Beauty calling unto Death.

Sleep knew that sound, and there immortal
  Christ rose out of the rock-tombed clod ;
And in its bright and vine-clad portal,
  At midnight stood the Son of God.

## ELIZABETH HENRY MILLER.

O distant Past ! whose shadows deepening round me,
    Hide from my view what once seemed bright and
      clear,
Thou canst not blur her image whose love crowned me,
    Whose spirit to my soul draws strangely near.

I know her quiet form is safely sleeping
    Beneath the watchful glance of Heaven's eye ;
I know the sound of my wild, bitter weeping,
    Cannot disturb her cold serenity.

And well I know her memory shall linger,
    Unheeding Time's imperious decree,
Till solemn Death shall lay his icy finger
    Upon my fettered soul and set it free.

JAMES C. MOFFAT.

(Class of " 1835.")

# EXTRACTS FROM "ALWYN."

[*From Canto I.*]

---

What recks to tell of birth and long descent ?
Is not the spirit from Jehovah sprung ?
Enough that Alwyn from his childhood bent
   Him to the toils of knowledge, and among
   The free, wild mountains was his fortune flung
Almost as free ; and lone and far away
   From all the bias of the babbling tongue,
His work conversed with Nature, and his play
Was o'er the learnèd page to linger night and day.

   *    *    *    *    *    *    *    *

Where streamlets, rushing down the mountain side,
   Leap in their giddy haste from lin to lin ;
And overhanging groves, in solemn pride
   And mystic twilight, shut their chorus in
   As with a temple, where the murmuring din,

With song of birds, half plaintive and half glad,
  The worship speak of those who cannot sin,
He oft would linger till their influence had
A kindred feeling wrought, as happy and as sad.

\*     \*     \*     \*     \*     \*     \*     \*

When summer morning crowned the hills with gold,
  And stretched their lengthened shadows o'er the
    plain,
When early shepherd, hastening to the fold,
  Or mountain ranges of his wild domain,
  Gave to the breeze his spirit-prompted strain,
'Twas to the enthusiast boy a draft of new
  And sweeter life the highest peak to gain,
Whence all the varied landscape, bursting through
The lower twilight, lay like pictures to his view:


The effulgent orb ascending from the deep
  Of nether space, bathed in a flood of light;
The dewy uplands, which all night did weep
  His absence, now rejoicing in the might
  Of his returning, tenderly as bright,
Like gladdened Beauty smiling in her tears;
  The obscure beyond—skirts of retreating night,
Which still upon the western verge appears,
Like half-defeated foe, yet struggling with his fears:

The snow-white mists along a hundred vales,
  Slumbering in silence by their hidden streams,
And as the invading day their rest assails,
  Slowly ascending on the advancing beams;
  While here and there some village coppice seems
An island in the flood of fleecy cloud
  Melting away before the warmth which teems
From yon triumphant orb, as if the proud
Earth had awoke from death and bondage of the
  shroud :

The voice of many waters, shining rills,
  Like living things in wilful song and play,
Which, by a thousand tiny falls, the hills
  Pour down into the glens; the ceaseless fray,
  Where adverse streams do battle for the way,
Their graver rush united, and the roar
  Of the fierce cataract, whose hoary spray
Is Nature's incense-cloud, and evermore
The distant river's dash upon its rocky shore;

And rising with the day the sweeter notes,
  Which draw their daily being from the sun,
The lark's clear matin hymn, which downward floats,
  As if in joy from heaven already won;

The long complaints, which o'er the mountains run,
From fleecy flocks descending from their lair,
   And far below, from labors re-begun,
The sounds of human life, rising like prayer,
Blend into sweet accord upon the throbbing air.

*    *    *    *    *    *    *    *

When Nature, panting with excess of life,
   Beneath the ripe luxuriance of noon,
Lavished her wealth on the broad landscape, rife
   With all the offspring of redundant June,
   Where sighing groves with murmuring brooks com-
      mune,
Where meadows wave, or fields of ripening grain,
   Vocal with insect being's drowsy tune,
Where listless herds bestrew the grassy plain,
Would Alwyn quaff the scene, till very bliss was pain.


But when, for many a long and burning day,
   The latest cloud had disappeared on high,
And the white, molten sun pursued his way
   Across the surface of a brazen sky,
   Bleaching the earth with unrelenting eye,
When withering pastures crumpled to the tread,
   And brooks exhaled had left their channels dry,

With panting herds he to the shelter fled,
And looked for Nature's death, as if her source were
dead.


Nor with less awe beheld the Titan war
Of the returning clouds, so long exiled,
Their angry hosts assembling from afar
In masses on the low horizon piled,
Where glorious light, with darkness reconciled,
Rested upon their crests, their armor lined.
But lo! they come, swift skirmishers and wild
Sweep o'er the sky, soon with the ranks combined,
And distant thunder rolls up solemnly behind.


And heavy drops fall far apart and slow,
Each on the sand a momentary stain.
The winds leap forth—an ambuscade—and lo!
The forest writhes and tosses as with pain,
The dust is swept in clouds along the plain.
Again the thunders issue their command,
And freely falls the cool, refreshing rain,
Copious, but gentle, and with teeming hand
Pours down new stores of life upon the fainting land.

Ye tranquil summer days, whose breath is balm,
　And soft as rising of the morning dew,
How little wot we that the child-like calm
　Which fills the soul with confidence in you,
　Is but a truce, the balance nice and true
Of such stupendous forces—deadly foes,
　Just waiting with the fatal aim in view,
Ready, when God permits, in strife to close,
Which shall this solid globe dissolve in mortal throes.

\* \* \* \* \* \* \* \*

[*From Canto II.*]

The Theban eagle, in his sunward flight,
　Alwyn pursued with charmed and eager eye,
Whether through darkening clouds, eluding sight,
　Or flashing out in evening's richest dye,
　Or in eternal truth's serenest sky
He soared in light, wooing the pure desire
　From earth's renown to nobler things on high.
Then o'er its ashes mourned the Cean fire,
The wreck of Lesbian song, and Sappho's broken
　　lyre.

How the heart gladdens in its own bright dream
　Of old Æolian and Doric song!

Bathed in the beauty of that lyric stream,
　Whose waves alone the history prolong,
　All nature smiles; that then were woe and wrong,
That then were irksome toils and cloudy days
　We overlook.　Like future to the young,
So 'to the classic taste the past conveys
Only the poet's world, the magic of his lays.


The joyous Melos seems to fill the air,
　The buoyant music of a sunny clime,
And Elegy, her sister, not less fair,
　With holy Dithyramb, in her sublime
　Religious ecstacy, blend with the chime
Of choral chants, and festive melodies
　The voice of Hellas, in her golden prime,
And Ceos, Lesbos, Thebes and Sparta rise
In Fancy's fairest light to Fancy's dazzled eyes.

\*　\*　\*　\*　\*　\*　\*　\*

[*From Canto VII.*]

Self-humbled son of God, atoning lamb
　Who once for men descendedst from thy throne,
How shall I praise Thee, sinful as I am,
　All holy as Thou art?　Through Thee alone
　Is God to man in love and mercy known.

In Thy commands all duty lies enshrined ;
  From beauty's full perfection hast Thou shone,
Thyself more fair than form of human kind,
And Thou alone hast peace to calm the troubled
    mind.


How ill we comprehend Thy word of life,
  And what laborious helplessness we prove ;
What wars we wage, what unavailing strife
  Within our souls to take Thy hand of love.
  Not by the path of learning must they move,
Not by the light of human wisdom see,
  Who would secure the wisdom from above.
Humbler the way, and briefer far must be—
Faith of the docile heart, which rests alone on Thee.


    *    *    *    *    *    *    *    *


What blessed transformations have been wrought
  By Thy so humble life, upon mankind ;
Hard-hearted men made tender, word and thought,
  The once polluted chaste, the coarse refined,
  The timid valiant, and the wavering mind
Fixed to one lofty purpose.  That which sums
  Up all the best in human life designed,
And all the grace that blesses happiest homes,
Spring up along the path by which Thy mercy comes.

For Thee has Genius wreathed the bay and palm,
  For Thee the sweetest harps on earth been strung,
Expectant harmonies of Hebrew psalm,
  And pre-ordained prophetic pæans sung.
  For Thee, before Thy wonderous birth, Thy young
And virgin mother raised the adoring strain.
  For Thee the gates of heaven were open flung,
And hymning angels, in long, choral train,
Issued with glorious song to hail Thy earthly reign.


A chorus worthy of a heavenly choir,
  A hymn to go resounding through all time,
Announced Thy birth in spirit of a higher
  Degree of being, and a holier clime.
  Thy life laborious, suffering, yet sublime,
In singleness, severity of aim,
  Though brief, and closed in early manhood's prime,
Beyond all measure of mere mortal fame,
An epic grander far than mind of man could frame.

K

# WITHOUT CHRIST.

O Christ, the world is dark—
    Ghostly dark for me;
And life would have no mark
    But for Thee.


I know not whence I came,
    Whither I must go.
Life wavers without aim,
    To and fro.


Nothing seems worth my love,
    Nothing worth my care;
All below, all above,
    Blank and bare.


To men my soul would close
    Her gates, and decline
Their contact, but for those
    Who are Thine.

This weary, hopeless heart
  In loneness would dwell
In the furthest, darkest part
  Of her cell.

And when near to life's brink,
  Would yield what it gave,
Without a word, and slink
  Into the grave.

There's nothing time can give,
  Nothing I could be,
For which 'tis worth to live
  But for Thee.

# THE BORDER OF THE WILDERNESS.

[*Authoress.*]

Towering heights of Ingall's River,
Fir-fringed crests of Mount Success,
Pine and birch and maple forests,
Border of the wilderness,—

Darkening in the evening glory,
Hiding in each wild ravine,
Depths of life, of mystic beauty,
Never yet by mortal seen :—

Still ye beckon, beckon ever,
Saying, " Come, our sister, come !
Quit the weary, glaring highways,
Seek within our shades a home.

" Firmly stands each rocky buttress,
Bears aloft scant growth of trees,
Deep beneath, sweet waters pouring,
Mingle music with the breeze.

" Come, O sister, come and rest thee !
    Thou and we are thoughts of God,
Friends alone thou'lt find among us,
    Friends who wield no critic's rod.

" If thy locks have lost their shining,
    Tresses grey our limbs adorn :
If thy brow be sadly furrowed,
    Wrinkled we ere thou wast born.

" If the young have ceased to love thee,
    Shun they too our awesome ways;
If thy steps have lost their fleetness,
    Stand we here these myriad days.

" Feel'st thy shadow darkening eastward,
    We against the twilight show,
But we know the dawn returneth,
    Wait with us that blessed glow."

HENRY J. VAN DYKE.

(Class of "1873.")

# THE WINGS OF A DOVE.

At sunset, when the rosy light was dying
  Swift down the pathway of the west,
I saw a lonely dove in silence flying
  To be at rest.

Emblem of peace, I cried, could I but borrow
  Thy pinions fleet, thy freedom blest,
I'd fly away from every careful sorrow
  And be at rest!

At twilight through the shadows softly falling,
  Back came the dove to seek her nest:
In the deep wood from which her mate was calling
  There was true rest.

Peace, heart of mine! no longer sigh to wander,
  Vex not thyself in fruitless quest,
There are no happy islands over yonder,—
  Come home and rest.

# THE AFTER–ECHO.

When the long echoes die away
Along the shores of silence, as a wave,
    Retreating, circles down the sand ;— .
When, one by one, with sweet delay
The mellow sounds that cliff and island gave
    Have lingered in the crescent bay,
    Until by lightest breezes fanned
    They float far off into the dying day,
    And all is still as death,
        Then listen ! Hark !—
    A slender wavering breath
    Comes from the borders of the dark,
    A note as clear and slow
    As falls from some enchanted bell,
Or spirit, passing from the world below
    That whispers back—Farewell.    ·
So in the heart
    When, slowly fading down the past,
    Fond memories depart,
    And each that leaves it seems the last,

Long after all the rest are gone,
Comes back a well-remembered tone,
  The after-echo of departed years,
  And touches all the soul to tears.

LYMAN WHITNEY ALLEN.

(Class of "1881.")

THEOLOGICAL SEMINARY.

# THE VENUS DI MILO.

[*From the Art-Cycle.*]

*There is never a path with its thorny way*
*Under heavy burdens our feet have trod,*
*But will bear the prints to endless day*
*Of the bleeding feet of the Son of God.*

—M. I.

Goddess of love, yet marble : warm, yet cold :
Speechless, yet speaking from thine earnest eyes :
Proud lips in nestling scorn and stern surprise,
Wreathing a smile o'er wealth of yearnful mould :
Bosom whose arching splendors full unfold
Slow heaving swells of slumbering sacrifice ;
Fair limbs imperious in their draped disguise
Shining through trembling spray of ocean old ;
Mysterious Goddess ! through thy marble form,
Wrought by the throes of toiling centuries,
The writhing spirit bursts the lifeless stone ;
Through the incarnate passion, deep and warm,
The human Infinite transcends the skies,
And sits enthroned on the eternal throne.

# THE MADONNA DEL SISTO.

[*From the Art-Cycle.*]

Virgin outwoven of God's prophecies !
Woman of earth-born race and heaven-worn face,
Rapt in majestic gladness and sweet grace,
  Stamping fair Christ upon the centuries ;—
  Eyes orient with Heaven's mysteries,
In frightened joy beaming triumphant praise ;
Lips breathing bliss of Christ's dear kiss the trace
  In widening curves of tremulous ecstasies.
  Beauty that baffles art ! Sweet heaven that bends
Earth to its knees with higher instincts wrought !
  Woman, that moulds the life of the wide years !
  Interpreter of Man ! through thee ascends,
Lifting vast worlds unto God's perfect thought,
  Love, the redeeming power that sways the spheres.

## CARL GUTHERZ' "ECCE HOMO."

O rare pale face! sacredly beautiful
With flowing locks of richest auburn hue—
A crown within a crown—whose ringlets strew
   Their silken wealth o'er brow most sorrowful;
   Fair eyes, from out whose azure pitiful
A pleading glory shines through crystal dew;
Sweet quivering lips that breathe a blessing new,
   In silent woe of love most tenderful.
   Lone-splendored Head, that bowed unto the tomb!
Thou risest in thy majesty divine,
Victorious o'er thy mighty agony.
   Thou thorn-crowned Christ! through the bewildering
      gloom,
Forevermore thy radiant face shall shine,
The beacon-light of Immortality.

# THE SONG OF THE HELL-SPIRIT.

I flew to the blossoming earth,
  And sipped of its honeyed flowers ;
I played in fierce joy and mirth
  Thro' the golden summer hours.
I sipped of the lily-bell
  From its white translucent cup,
But a red stain on it fell
  And drank all the whiteness up.


I sat on the sandy shore
  And played with the feathery spray ;
I dived 'neath the waste sea's roar,
  Where the sunbeams never stray.
But the silver waves grew red,
  Like the blood of some monster slain ;
And over their ocean-bed
  Hoarsely murmured their sad refrain.


I sped through the ebon night,
  Through the realms of the trembling stars

To the whirling orbs of light
  In their golden orient cars.
But the shining mists grew dim,
  While the moon waxed fiery red,
And o'er the horizon's brim
  Its baleful effulgence spread.


I soared till my wearied wings
  Poised high o'er the gates of light,
Where the great World-Spirit sings
  Through the darkling Infinite;
But the song hushed to a moan
  That thrilled thro' the fretted space,
And a glistening tear-drop shone
  On a pale and upturned face.

# ALAS.

My heart is sad with waiting, Love,
  Waiting for thee;
My eyes are dim with watching, Love,
  Watching for thee.
The sunlight fades, the night draws nigh,
The stars come forth in the clear sky,
I sit alone,—alone, and sigh,
  Sighing for thee.

My heart is faint with longing, Love,
  Longing for thee;
My eyes are worn with weeping, Love,
  Weeping for thee.
The night winds murmur as they pass
Trailing thy name through the long grass;
My soul cries out, alas! alas!
  Alas for me!

CORNELIA PEARSON.

# SCENE IN A STUDIO.

[*Authoress of " Wreaths and Branches."*]

A distinguished sculptor destroyed some of his finest works, that
they might not fall into the hands of an inexorable creditor.

'Tis midnight, yet a flickering torch still gleams
Within the sculptor's studio, whose light
Gives a new beauty to those forms of grace,
The emanations of a master mind,
And called to life by his creative power.
The artist grasps his chisel, but the glow
That mantles high upon his brow is not
The fire of new-born inspiration,
For Prometheus' self ne'er wore a look
Of such despairing agony.   Oh! sure
It were a glorious thing to people earth
With thoughts made palpable, and chaining thus
The lightning-fire of heaven, bid it flash forth
From lip and brow, instinct with Majesty !
Yes: Genius is a gift unparalleled,
But guarded round with fearful swords of flame,
That foot profane tread not the hallowed ground.

But what is this?   Has frenzy seized his brain?
Quick falls the mallet, not with well-aimed stroke
To guide the skillful chisel, and perfect
The fair proportions.—Stay thy hand, rash man!
Comes there no voice from this, the beauteous child
Of thy creative thought, which cries, "Forbear!"
One hour of madness must not thus destroy
The labour of thy ripened years.


'Tis done!   The shivering marble falls around
The woe-bewildered man, who gazes now
With tearless eye upon that martyred one,
Whose shapeless trunk but seems his agony
To mock: yet onward recklessly he goes,
And all the beauteous ones that he had loved
The Venus fair, the Manes of ancient gods,
The bust of heroes, and the dream-like ones
With their life's fountain faintly gushing forth
From out the stricken rock, at his command
All—all must perish!
O ruin dire! yet, sadder still the wreck
Of mind, which misery hath wrought.

# A PARTING WORD.

Written on her death-bed two hours before she died.

A parting word—if power were mine,
What most I value should be thine,
The brightest gem in diadem
     To deck thy brow,
The fairest flower in garden bower,
     I'd gather now.
The Pearl of Price, that gem should be
The thornless Rose, my gift to thee.

L

## THE VEIL OF THE SPIRIT.

The face is the veil of the spirit,
  Worn strangely two worlds between,
And until at death it be lifted,
  The wearer shall never be seen.


We meet, and we talk, and we linger,
  We mix with women and men ;
But the soul, after all is over,
  Makes only a sign now and then.


And the sign is that of a shadow
  Cast through a doubtful screen :
Ah ! the only things that we ever see
  Are the things that are all unseen.

# THE TWO CITIES.

[*From Littell's Living Age.*]

By the city of the living,
　By its ceaseless toil and tread,
So fair and so forgiving,
　Stands the city of the dead.
Like twins, in a rocking cradle,
　They lie in the darkness deep,
And one is awake with a fever,
　But the other is—asleep.


Side by side rise the two great cities,
　Afar on the traveller's sight :
One, black with the dust of labor,
　One, solemnly still and white.
Apart, and yet together,
　They are reached in a dying breath,
But a river flows between them,
　And the river's name is—Death.


Anon, from the hut and the palace,
　Anon, from early till late,

They come rich and poor together
   Asking alms at thy beautiful gate.
And never had life a guerdon
   So welcome to all to give,
In the land where the living are dying,
   As the land where the dead may live.


And thus the two great cities
   Of the living and the dead,
Stand side by side in their shadow,
   And the river flows on in its bed.
But the river leans a little
   Under the further brink;
And I love to lean with the river
   To that shaded side—and think.


In one there is soft-winged slander,
   And rumour of windy deeds;
In the other a well-kept secret,
   And a riddle that nobody reads.
In one they are bitterly turning
   Their faces in anger away;
In the other they meet for forgiveness,
   Face to face in the blinding clay.

In one the lights are burning
    In the window and the street,
For a thousand forms returning,
    For a thousand eager feet.
In the other the lights of Heaven
    Gleam down through the mist of doubt ;
And the virgin stars are shining
    For the lamps that have all gone out.


O silent City of refuge !
    On the way to the city o'erhead,
The gleam of thy marble milestones
    Tells the distance we are from the dead.
Full of feet, but a city untrodden ;
    Full of hands, but a city unbuilt ;
Full of strangers who know not even
    That their life-cup lies there spilt.


They know not the tomb from the palace,
    They dream not they ever have died :
God be thanked they never will know it
    Till they live on the other side.
From the doors that death shut coldly
    On the face of their last lone woe,
They came to thy glades for shelter,
    Who had nowhere else to go.

They sought thy quiet slumber
   With a strange and wingèd haste :
As a wrecking ship in the tempest
   An isle, in the billowy waste.
They fled to thy sable forest
   As dust is blown by the breeze ;
When the little children, frightened,
   Run out of the rain, under trees.


O city of the Silent !
   What a world lies in your spell,
What an army of pale-face pilgrims
   Encamped in yon white-tented dell.
Like the dark room in the household,
   Thick with cobwebs, and mould and rust,
And filled with old-fashioned remnants,
   Is thy dark room of the dust.


Creation is God's cenotaph
   Above Christ's unstoned grave ;
Unmarked of shaft or marble,
   Unsung of wind or wave.
And 'mid all the glittering planets
   That fling their crowns on space,
Earth is the only star that holds
   Their monarch's resting-place.

Shall the flower come up forever?
    And daisy and buttercup
Catch part of God's smile off in heaven,
    And never a soul come up?
E'en now they are teaching us thither,
    As nurses teach children to walk;
And I hear their sweet tones, Come up hither,
    And the air is full of their talk.


And I feel as I fall to thinking
    That my face is dusty with death:
I may wash it with sleep for a moment,
    But it settles again with my breath.
And I know that I soon shall mingle
    With those whose footsteps are fled,
Who dwell in the crowded city,—
    The city of the dead.


O grave! where is thy victory?
    O death! where is thy sting?
And what is thy raven shadow
    But the shadow of a wing?
And what if the dead hear nothing
    Beneath the closèd door;
Since we who listen in open space
    If we hear, hear nothing more.

# ·  GRADUATION  SONG.

Ho, students ! come out !
Swarm here on this mellow old sod, where for years,
In these hours of suspense we have cheated our tears,
With hopes, reminiscences, songs, ringing cheers :—
　　　Hasten out.


Join your hands, clear the brow,
'Tis the hour for our fond Alma Mater to wean
Her young brood of the year; oh ! how often in vain,
Shall we yearn for her wing of protection again,
　　　In this nest.


Dear nest, oh ! how calm
Will it seem, when life's tempests shall gather and beat
Cold, fierce and remorseless : and manhood must meet,
　　　Oh, how calm.


And yet here, where we stand,
Aye, on this very sod which we press, unconcerned,
How many brave breasts to the future have turned—

How many have grasped her vain promise and burned
    For the strife.


    And where are they now ?
Some petted by fortune, some brilliant, some great,
With their names on the roll and their voice in the state,
Yet with gnawings unsatisfied, chafing at fate
    Evermore.


    Aye ! where are they now ?
Some wasted, forgotten, some outcast, some gone ;
Life's solemn procession sweeps endlessly on ;
Are we ready to join it ?  Probation is done,
    It is late.


    Farewell, boys, farewell.
May we all meet again in our Summer of life ;
In its Autumn, subdued and instructed by strife ;
In its Winter of age and repose, ere the knife
    Cuts us down.


    And, mother, farewell :
The gusts thro' the halls pass away with a sigh ;
Your breezes embrace, as the last moments fly,
The branches above wave a silent good-bye,
    So farewell.

# TO ———.

Authoress of a volume of unpublished Poems.

O were I yonder star, my love!
And thou beneath my beam shouldst stray,
How brightly would I smile above,
    To light thee on thy lonely way!

O were I, sweet, but zephyr now!
Fresh wafted from the balmy west,
I'd lay my touch upon thy brow,
    And hover round thy fevered rest.

O were I yonder bird so gay!
And thou within my shaded bower
I'd sing my sweetest roundelay
    To soothe thy spirit's troubled hour.

O were I but a rose so fair!
Within thy bosom thus to lie,
I'd breathe my sweetest odors there,
    To mingle with thy faintest sigh.

# E. A. K.

[*By a Lady.*]

## A FRAGMENT.

For ah, did the angel of peace ever roam
On an errand of love from her beautiful home,
She hath certainly paused in her holy career,
And folded her pinions enchantingly here;
Dear to me are thy shades where no sound may be heard,
Save the soul-soothing strains of thy harmonist bird,
For they seem on the soft wing of quiet to come,
Like ethereal melodies luring us home,—
Faint breathings from heaven, to bid us prepare,
For peals of celestial minstrelsy there.


But oh! when day rests on the portals of eve,
As tho' loth the bright scene of enchantment to leave;
While its drapery of gold hurried carelessly on,
Fades away, tint by tint, till at last all are gone;
Methinks, 'tis an emblem of life's little hour,
Thus perish the hues of hope's loveliest flower,
And sigh for repose on that heavenly shore,
Where the day is eternal, and change is no more.

## TO —— :.

Though short the time since our first meeting,
 And I must now prepare to part,
Those interviews, so sweet, so fleeting,
 Have left their impress on my heart;


And though thy heart is naught affected,
 And I may soon forgotten be,
To love—though but to be rejected,—
 Is all the fate that's left for me.


Long years ago, a bird who wended
 Her way to some far-distant land,
Upon a river's bank descended
 And left her foot-print on the sand.


Lightly she rose and left the river,
 And onward kept her thoughtless way,
The sand she pressed forgets her never,
 And hard rock bears her print to-day.

Thus will my heart, till its warm beatings
　Are stilled fore'er in death's cold shade,
Cherish the memory of our meetings,
　And keep the impress thou hast made.

# ONLY A CURL.

One little curl of golden hair,
Yet how many memories centre there!
Of deep blue eyes so soft, so bright,
Now melting in love, now laughing in light,
Sweet founts whence the crystal tears would flow
Unbidden at every tale of woe.
Ah! why are those bright eyes gleaming there
In that little curl of golden hair!


It brings back cheeks that mocked the rose,
And the brow that was whiter than winter snows,
And the smiling lip and the dimpled chin
That told of the joyous heart within,
And the little hand that in his would rest
Like the trembling bird in her hidden nest,
In those days that knew not of sorrow or care,—
All these are seen in that curl of hair.


It recalls the arbor beneath whose shade
True love was breathed and fond vows were made,

And the shadowy lane where oft they roved
In the twilight hour by the poet loved,
And the dear old house in the distant town,
(Strangers have long ago torn it down,)
But they can't destroy it, it lingers there
In that little curl of her beautiful hair.

It whispers of love so fond and true,  ·
And the look that told him that she loved too,
And the sweet betrothal, when from her brow
He cut the lock that's before him now,
And the fatal day that saw them part,
And a black-sealed letter—a broken heart.
Love and hope, and woe and despair,
All are told by that golden hair.

The present has vanished, the past is here
With its scenes so happy, its forms so dear.
From out the dark tomb's dismal hall
That little curl has brought them all.
One little curl of golden hair,
And all that he ever has loved is there.

# "I AM FREE."

"I am free," laughs the stream, as all rippling and leaping
    O'er rock and through meadow it speeds on its way,
Now dancing in sunlight, in shadow now sleeping
    Now foaming and angry, now sparkling and gay.
The stream may flow on till it swell to a river,
    May wind as it will, and may say "I am free,"
But the voice of the oceansurge calls it forever,
    And however it flow, it must flow to the sea.


"I am free," sings the air, "and no power can constrain
    me
    To wind in a valley, or flow to a sea,
No banks can enclose me, no barriers restrain me,
    Of all of earth's creatures I only am free."
But a chain all unseen ever fetters its motion,
    And back to the earth holds its uprising wing,
It may sigh thro' the forest or roar on the ocean,
    It may sweep round the earth, but to earth it must
    cling.

" We are free," shout the comets, as in their wild courses
   They fly in derision by planets and stars,
While out in bright flame stream the manes of the
    horses
   That hurry through æther their luminous cars.
The comet may rush to the verge of creation,
   Far beyond our weak vision its course it may run,
But still it obeys the strong hand, Gravitation,
   And again in its course 'twill return to the sun.


" I am free," cries the spirit of Youth, "on strong pinion
   Where'er my gay fancy may list I can rove;"
But one power still maintains an unbroken dominion,
   'Tis the soul's gravitation—the sweet force of love.
The sea whose sweet musical voices e'er call me,
   My earth and my sun are all centred in thee,
From their sweet strong attractions that ever enthrall
    me
   I am not, and Oh! may I never be free!
M

# A FRAGMENT.

*   *   *   *   *   *   *   *

But when the idol of my heart's devotion
   I think to seize and bind with memory's chain,
Striving to reach it, mad with fond emotion,
   It flies, and I sink back to toil and pain;
As some lost swimmer on a stormy ocean
   Looks on the distant lights he ne'er can gain,
And sinks to death murmuring a once loved name.

# A LOST SOUL.

I met a soul at midnight far out upon the deep,
It dreamed not with my dreaming, it slept not with my
sleep;
A face that I had met on earth, a face that once was
fair,
I saw it, and it wore the wild worn beauty of despair.

I asked it of the tearless grief that gathered to its eye,
I asked it of that calm despair, that death that ne'er can
die.
I asked it whither it was bound, what countries it had
crossed;
It pointed to Eternity, and only answered—Lost.

Else answerless, it floated by upon the midnight air,
Till, like the gliding of a ghost its spirit was not there;
I rose to follow it—I woke—O God! that soul was
mine,
The shadow of that dream may fall upon some sleep of
thine.

Some startled sleep amid the night of life's entrancing
 ease,
That takes the sleeper to its breast, that leaves him on
 his knees ;
And if it come, O scorn it not, however light it seem :
Men have been saved ere this within the passing of a
 dream.


O to be lost in such a night or wrecked on such a sea,
No port,—no light,—no shore,—no God ;—naught but
 Eternity,
To sob along the outer wall forever unforgiven,
Whose inner arches ring with all the happiness of heaven.

## "WE WERE FRIENDS TOGETHER."

*[Authoress of "Poems."]*

We were friends, gay friends, together,
  And a strange, deep gloom is shed
On the memories that wither
  Since I feel that thou art dead.
Many a dear and cherished token
  Of our youth's too cloudless dawn,
Is all ruined now, and broken
  In my heart, for thou art gone.


We were friends, when joy's light measure
  From life's golden harp was rung,
And the ripening fruits of pleasure
  All along our pathway hung.
When no glad warm thought repressing
  Heart and soul laughed from our eyes,
As the light of God's own blessing
  Laughs in sunshine from the skies.

When the present was too cheerful
   To regret a pleasure past,
Or to tremble and be fearful
   That they would not always last.
E're we learned that all too often
   In the fairest blossom's cup,
(Tho' its tints the south winds soften,)
   There is poison folded up.


We were friends, when every feeling
   Was as warm and pure and bright
As the summer air when reeling
   'Neath a weight of amber light.
And as tuneful as the gushes
   Of some merry little stream,
When the wind steals thro' the rushes
   On its dimpled breast to dream.


In a southern clime we wandered,
   And thro' gardens whose perfume
Crowds of regal roses squandered
   From their treasuries of bloom.
And where starry myrtles quivered
   'Neath the kisses of the spring,
Pure as flakes of snow dissever
   From the white cloud's spotless wing.

There by moonlight of't we revelled,
  Or, when morning's orient crown,
Like an angel's hair dishevelled,
  From the blue sky floated down.
In rich waves of sunlight weeping,
  When magnolia's blooms were seen,
Like a flock of white doves peeping
  From their hermitage of green.


We were friends when smiles of gladness
  Lit thy boyhood's stately home,
E're we dreamed that so much sadness
  There in after years would come.
Many dwelt at that proud manor,
  Yet no heir is left to claim
Or to spread the stainless honor
  Of an old and cherished name.


But tho' brief our summer meeting,
  Thou art only gone before,
And my spirit sends thee greeting
  To that far-off Eden shore,
Where the dews of youth still glisten,
  And sweet fancies seem to tell
That thine angel·ear will listen
  To the voice of my farewell.

## RECOMPENSE.

*[Authoress.]*

---

In a still and beauteous bower,
Gemmed with many a lovely flower,
Where the sun is shining brightly—
Where the zephyrs, playing lightly,
Whisper words of tenderest love,
From the blessed world above ;
There, a prisoner, sigheth one !
'Mid this beauty, she alone
Weeps the passing hours away,
Longing for the close of day ;
There—in solitary state,
A lone bird sighing for its mate.


Not for her the sun is shining !
Not for her these flowers twining !
Words of love the zephyrs sing,
But no cheer for her they bring !
Who are they that dwell above ?

What know they of pain or love?
What to her that beauteous bower?
Welcome, blighting wind and shower,
Droop your heads, ye flowers of spring,
And ye birds, forget to sing.
Aught but dirge for her sad fate,
A lone bird, sighing for its mate!


But lo! at evening's gentle close
A nightingale's sweet song arose
So subtle was this wondrous song
No human voice could give it tongue
A voice from regions of the blest,
A song of weariness at rest,
Tones from a heart where all is peace,
And perfect love that cannot cease:
Where love and care and grief have striven,
There reigneth now the bliss of heaven;
The lone bird only sings so late—
A love bird singing to its mate.

GEORGE W. BETHUNE.

THEOLOGICAL SEMINARY.

# IT IS NOT DEATH TO DIE.

[*Author of " Poems."*]

It is not death to die,
  To leave this weary road,
And 'mid the brotherhood on high
  To be at home with God.


It is not death to close
  The eye long dimmed by tears,
And wake in glorious repose
  To spend eternal years.


It is not death to bear
  The wrench that sets us free
From prison-bars, to breathe the air
  Of boundless liberty.

It is not death to fling
　Aside this sinful dust,
And rise on strong, exulting wing,
　To live among the just.


Jesus! Thou Prince of life!
　Thy chosen cannot die;
Like thee they conquer in the strife,
　To reign with thee on high.

# THE STRIFE OF THE ANGELS.

Within its downy cradle there lay a little child,
And a group of hovering angels unseen upon her smiled,
When a strife arose among them—a holy, loving strife,
Which should shed the richest blessing upon the new-
born life.


One breathed upon her features, and the babe in beauty
grew,
With a cheek like morning blushes, and an eye of azure
hue,
Till every one who saw her was thankful for the sight
Of a face so sweet and radiant with ever fresh delight.


Another gave her accents and a voice as musical
As a spring-bird's joyous carol or a rippling streamlet's
fall,
Till all who heard her laughter or her words of childish
grace,
Loved as much to listen to her as to look into her face.

Another brought from Heaven a clear and gentle mind,
And within the lovely casketing the precious gem en-
shrined,
Till all who knew her wondered that God should be so
good
As to bless with such a spirit a world so cold and rude.

Thus did she grow in beauty, in melody and truth,
The budding of her childhood just opening into youth,
And to our hearts yet dearer each moment than before,
She became, though we tho't fondly we could not love
her more.

Then out spake another angel, all brighter than the rest,
As with strong arm, yet tender, he caught her to his
breast,
Ye have made her all too lovely for a child of mortal
race,
But no shade of human sorrow shall darken her fair
face.

Ye have tuned to gladness only the accents of her tongue,
And no wail of human anguish shall from her lips be
wrung;
Nor shall the soul that shineth so purely from within
That form of earth-born frailty ever know a sense of sin.

Lulled in my faithful bosom, I will bear her far away,
Where there is no sin nor anguish, no sorrow or decay ;
And mine a boon more glorious than all your gifts shall
    be,
Lo ! I crown her happy spirit with Immortality.


Then on his heart our darling yielded up her gentle
    breath,
For the stronger, brighter angel, who loved her best
    was—Death.

# NIGHT STUDY.

I am alone—and yet
In the still solitude there is a rush
Around me, as were met
A crowd of viewless wings, I hear a gush
Of mystic harmonies—heaven meeting earth,
Making it to rejoice with holy mirth.

Ye winged phantasies,
Sweeping before my spirit's conscious eye,
Calling me to arise,
To go forth with you from my very self and fly
Far into the unseen, unknown Immense
Of worlds beyond our sphere, what are ye?   Whence?

Ye eloquent voices,
Now soft as breathings of a distant lute,
Now strong as when rejoices
The trumpet in the victory and pursuit;
Strange are ye, yet familiar, as ye call
My soul to wake from earth's sense and its thrall.

I know ye now—I see
With more than natural sight.  Ye are the good,
    The wise departed.  Ye
Are come from Heaven to claim your brotherhood
With mortal brother writhing in the strife
And chains, which once were yours in this sad life.

    Ye hover o'er the page
Ye traced in ancient days with glorious thought,   .
    Full many a distant age;
Ye love to watch the inspiration caught
From your sublime examples, and to cheer
The fainting student to your high career.

    Ye come to nerve the soul
(Like him who near the Atoner stood when He,
    Trembling, saw round him roll
The wrathful portents of Gethsemane)
With courage strong; the promise ye have known
And proved, wrapt for me from the Eternal Throne.

    Still keep, O keep me near you,
Compass me round with your immortal wings;
    Still let my glad soul hear you,
Striking your triumphs from your golden strings,
Until with you I mount and join the song
An angel like you 'mid the white-robed throng.

# DR. BETHUNE'S LAST HYMN.

Written on his dying bed.

Published for the first time.

When time seems short, and death is near,
And I am pressed by doubt and fear,
And sins like an o'erflowing tide
Assail my peace on every side,
This thought my refuge still shall be,
I know the Saviour died for me.

His name is Jesus, and he died
For guilty sinners—crucified—
Content to die that he might win
Their ransom from the death of sin.
No sinner worse than I can be,
Therefore I know he died for me.

If grace were bought, I could not pay,
If grace were earned, no worth have I,
By grace alone I draw my breath,
Held up from everlasting death.

N

Yet since I know his grace is free,
I know the Saviour died for me.


I read God's holy word, and find
Great truths which elevate my mind,
And little do I know beside,
Of thoughts so high, so deep, so wide.
This is my best Theology—
I know the Saviour died for me.

## ANNIS BOUDINOT STOCKTON.

Author of "The Triumph of Mildness."

---

*Excerpt from a Letter addressed to her by Gen. Washington:*

Rocky Hill, Sept. 2d, 1783.

You apply to me, my dear madam, for absolution, as though I were your father confessor. If it is a crime to write elegant poetry, and if you will come and dine with me on Thursday, and go through the proper course of penitence, I will strive hard to acquit you of your poetical trespasses.

Your most obedient and obliged servant,

Geo. Washington.

Mrs. Stockton.

---

# ODE TO WASHINGTON.

---

With all thy country's blessings on thy head,
And all the glory that encircles man,
Thy deathless fame to distant nations spread,
And realms unblest by Freedom's genial plan ;
Addressed by statesmen, legislators, kings,
Revered by thousands as you pass along,
While every muse with ardor spreads her wings,
To greet our hero in immortal song:
Say, can a woman's voice an audience gain,

And stop a moment thy triumphal car?
And wilt thou listen to a peaceful strain,
 Unskilled to paint the horrid wrack of war?
For what is glory?   What are martial deeds,
 Unpurified at Virtue's awful shrine?
Full oft remorse a glorious day succeeds—
 The motive, only, stamps the deed divine.
But thy last legacy, renownèd chief,
 Hath decked thy brow with honors more sublime—
Twined in thy wreath, the Christian's firm belief,
 And nobly owned thy faith to future time.

# MY ROCK.

I lay upon the rocky strand,
 The Atlantic breaking at my feet,
And smiled, and laved my idle hand
 Where sea and rock in thunder meet.

With cannon peal, through misty smoke,
 At me its volleyed waters flew :
Ye harm me, O ye seas, I spoke,
 But as the flowers are harmed by dew.

It heard, and from its deepest bed
 It summoned all the boundless main,
And roaring came ; I merely said :
 Go, gather for th' assault again !

My little life it fiercer sought,
 With hungry howl and angry leap ;
Its madness was to music wrought,
 Which lulled me into childlike sleep.

I slept, and woke, and laughed to see
  Such fearful force but spent in foam,
And scoffed—Your wrath but proves to me
  My Rock is my sufficient home.

.

# WILLIAM W. LORD.

(CLASS OF "1843.")

THEOLOGICAL SEMINARY.

(*Author of two volumes of Poems.*)

## A RIME.

[*From Griswold's "American Poets."*]

[Which is yet Reason, and teacheth in a light manner a grave matter in the lore of love.]

---

As Love sat idling beneath a tree,
A knight rode by on his charger free,
Stalwart and fair and tall was he
With his plume and his mantle, a sight to see!
And proud of his scars, right loftily
He cried, Young boy, will you go with me?
But Love, he pouted and shook his head,
And along fared the warrior ill-bested;
    Love is not won by chivalry.


Then came a minstrel bright of blee,
Blue were his eyes as the heavens be,

And sweet as a song-bird's throat sang he
Of smiles and tears and ladies e'e,
Soft love and glorious chivalry.
Then cried, Sweet boy, will you go with me?
Love wept and smiled and shook his head,
And along fared the minstrel ill-bested;
    Love is not won by minstrelsy.


Then came a bookman wise as three,
Darker a scholar you shall not see,
In Jewry, Rome, or Araby.
But list, fair dames, what I rede to ye,
In love's sweet lore untaught was he.
For when he cried, Come, love, with me!
Tired of the parle he was nodding his head,
And along fared the scholar ill-bested;
    Love is not won by pedantry.


Then came a courtier wearing the key
Of council and chambers high privity.
He could dispute yet seem to agree,
And soft as dew was his flatterie.
And with honied voice and low congee,
Fair youth, he said, will you honor me?

In courteous wise Love shook his head,
And along fared the courtier ill-bested ;
 Love is not won by courtesy.


Then came a miser blinking his e'e,
To view the bright boy beneath the tree ;
His purse, which hung to his cringing knee,
The ransom held of a king's countree,
And a handful of jewels and gold showed he,
And cried, Sweet boy, will you go with me?
Then loud laughed Love as he shook his head,
And along fared the monger ill-bested ;
 Love is not won by merchandry.


O then to young Love beneath the tree,
Came one as young and as fair as he,
And as like to him as like could be,
And clapping her little wings for glee,
With nods and smiles and kisses free,
She whispered, Come, O come with me.
Love pouted and flouted and shook his head,
But along with that winsome youth he sped,
 And love wins love, loud shouted she.

# THE PRINCESS LOUISE: THE MAIDEN ALL FOR–LORNE!

A blushing rose of England's crown,
Mingling with Scotia's thistle-down,
Shall tie of race and throne restore,
Through the great chief MacCallum More;
And noble blood of Briton born,
Shall wed the maiden all for-lorne.


God shower his blessings on the pair,
The Highland lad, the Lowland fair;
And grant the maiden all for-lorne,
May'nt marry a man all tattered and torn;
But Love with his own magic art
Blend princely natures heart to heart,
Forging meantime 'neath rosy smiles,
A chain to bind the British Isles.

GEORGE H. BOKER.

(Class of "1842.")

*Author of " Plays and Poems," " The Legend of the Hounds,"
" Poems," &c.*

## THE BLACK REGIMENT.

Dark as the clouds of even
Ranked in the western heaven,
Waiting the breath that lifts
All the dread mass, and drifts
Tempest and falling brand
Over a ruined land :—
So still and orderly,
Arm to arm, knee to knee,
Waiting the great event,
Stands the Black Regiment.

Down the long, dusky line
Teeth gleam and eye-balls shine :
And the bright bayonet,
Bristling, and firmly set,

Flashed with a purpose grand
Long e're the sharp command
Told them their time had come,
Told them what work was sent
For the Black Regiment.


" Now " the flag-sergeant cried !
" Though death and hell betide,
Let the whole nation see
If we are fit to be
Free in this land : or bound
Down, like the whining hound
Bound with red stripes of pain
In our old chains again ! "
O ! what a shout there went
From the Black Regiment !


" Charge ! " Trump and drum awoke
Onward the bondmen broke :
Bayonet and sabre-stroke
Vainly opposed their rush
Through the wild battle crush,
With but one thought aflush
Driving their lords like chaff,
In the gun's mouth they laugh,

Or at the slippery brands
Leaping with slippery hands;
Down they tear man and horse,
Down in their awful course,
Trampling with bloody heel
Over the crashing steel,
All their eyes forward bent,
Rushed the black Regiment.


"Freedom!" their battle-cry,
"Freedom! or leave to die."
Ah! and they meant the word,
Not as with us 'tis heard,
Not a mere party shout,
They gave their spirits out,
Trusted the end to God,
And on the gory sod
Rolled in triumphant blood;
Glad to strike one free blow,
Whether for weal or woe;
Glad to breathe one free breath,
Though on the lips of death;
Praying, alas, in vain,
That they might fall again,
So they could once more see
That burst to Liberty—

This was what Freedom meant
To the Black Regiment.


Hundreds on hundreds fell,
But they are resting well ;
Scourges and shackles strong
Never shall do them wrong.
O to the living few—
Soldier, be just, be true !
Hail them as comrades tried ;
Fight with them side by side ;
Never, in field or tent,
Scorn the Black Regiment.

# DIRGE FOR A SOLDIER.

To Gen. Phil. Kearney.   Killed Sept. 1st, 1862.

Close his eyes, his work is done!
    What to him is friend or foeman,
Rise of moon or set of sun,
    Hand of man or kiss of woman?
Lay him low, lay him low,
In the clover or the snow;
What cares he?   He cannot know—
    Lay him low.


As man may, he fought his fight,
    Proved his truth by his endeavor;
Let him sleep in solemn night,
    Sleep, forever and forever.
Lay him low, lay him low,
In the clover or the snow;
What cares he?   He cannot know—
    Lay him low.

Fold him in his country's stars,
  Roll the drum and fire the volley,
What to him are all earth's wars,
  What—but death-bemocking folly?
Lay him low, lay him low,
In the clover or the snow;
What cares he?   He cannot know—
  Lay him low.


Leave him to God's watchful eye;
  Trust him to the Hand that made him;
Mortal love weeps idly by;
  God alone hath power to aid him.
Lay him low, lay him low,
In the clover or the snow;
What cares he?   He cannot know—
  Lay him low.

## BEAUTIFUL SUNLIGHT.

Beautiful sunlight! Shadow of God,
Gleam from the sky where the glorified trod,
Still shining as once over Eden it shone,
Glory swept down from the great golden throne.

Beautiful sunlight! How dreary the day
Without thy bright spangles, like children at play,
Filling the sorrowful households of earth
With flame-winged angels of heavenly birth.

Beautiful sunlight! How deftly thy hand
Like an artist is painting the sky and the land;
Now crimsoning the swift cloud with roseate hue,
Now chasing the rainbow in orange and blue.

Now opening the lily, now touching the star,
Now brightening the dream of the distance afar,
Now washing the windows of night with its wave,
Now decking with beauty the gloom of the grave.

O

Thou walkest like God through the dust and the rain,
But thy silver-tipped sandals catch never a stain,
And though tempest and shadow wear over thy face,
It shows not a wrinkle, it bears not a trace.


O Light! what is light to the eyes of the blind
But a darkness whose pathway no traveller can find?
And what is the light of thy spirit to thee,
If that light be but darkness, how dark it must be!


O Father of lights, open thou these sealed eyes!
As windows in summer to stars in the skies;
To the beautiful prophecies shining on high,
"Show us the Father" and then we will die.

# TO A LOST CANARY.

Whither are thou fled, my birdie,
  Whither wings thy way ?
By the forest or the river,
  O'er the ocean's spray ?
Whither art thou fled, my birdie,
  Little birdie, say ?                .


Can it be, my pet canary,
  Of the plumaged breast,
Flitting like a yellow sunbeam
  From the saffron west,
Pines among dull-feathered woodsters
  In a common nest ?


O'er thy head perchance there hovers
  Hawk of angry sky ;
On thee now, mayhap, the fowler
  Fasteneth his eye ;
Wherefore didst thou leave thy mistress,
  Wherefore didst thou fly ?

Ah! thou'rt not the only nestling
  That hath flown from me,
Other friends as fair and lovely
  Left me lone like thee;
And I know not, O I know not
  Wheresoe'er they be.


But I know in yon bright Heaven,
  Far beyond the west,
Lie the mild Canary Islands,
  Islands of the Blest;
And some day I too shall fly
  Away—and be at rest.

GEORGE L. RAYMOND.

(Class of " ".)

*Author of " Colony Ballads," "Hadyn,"
" Life Below," &c.*

## NOTES FROM THE VICTORY.

Ah me! who is ringing those bells?
Right merry for funeral knells!
If wild winds fell, ring them thro' hell,
What woe can the demons lack?
My light blew out, in the gust of the rout:
My boy will never come back.


Drums too,—who bade the drums roll?
Coarse drums, call ye the soul?
Folks out of breath, shout ye at death?
Rend ye the tomb?—Alack.
Vain echoe's around, still, under the ground,
My boy can never come back.


And guns! What makes the guns roar?
Alas, I thought it was o'er!

Though why fear I, though millions die,
Though all of us wear but black?
I, too, with the proud have my blood-stained
    shroud ;
My boy will never come back.


Our land!—who wants its long years?
They are dimm'd by these drainless tears :
All gloom is the way of this masked grief-gay,
Who groans in their lonely track ;
Chill, shivering breast, freeze, freeze into rest;
My boy can never come back.

# THE DESTINY-MAKER.

She paused, and I who questioned there,
Heard that she was as good as fair :
And in my soul a still, small voice
Did chide because I checked my choice ;
But I who had resolved to bo
The maker of my destiny,
I bade the gentle guardian down,
And tried to think about renown.


She passed ; and I who lingered there,
Saw that her face was very fair ;
And with my sighs that pride suppressed
Fluttered a weary wish for rest ;
But I who had resolved to be
The maker of my destiny,
I turned me to my task and wrought,
And so forgot the passing thought.


She left :—and I who wander, fear
There's nothing more to see or hear :

Those walls that ward my Paradise
Are very high, now open twice ;
And I, who had resolved to be
The maker of my destiny,
Can only wait without the gate
And sit and sigh.   Too late! too late!

# THE RAPIDS AT NIAGARA.

*[Allaire.]*

Swift water-serpents ; with dread fascination,
   Upon me unnumbered ye dartingly glide ;
As strong as the power of some awful temptation,
   That lures me to merge in its tragical tide.


When I grew tired of the Cataract's thunder,
   Sank down to sleep 'neath the muffled-crowned mist,
Why was it, then, that ye rapt me with wonder,
   On your weird spell that I could not resist ?


Ah ! in those torrents my life flows before me,
   Far from its home in the quiet of years ;
Wrecks of my childhood drift brokenly o'er me,
   Dashed with strange visions of laughter and tears.


Once, far away where your swift waters started,
   Calm was their song as their own mountain spring ;
Alas ! how they lie on these rocks broken-hearted,
   And the song of my life is the song that they sing.

Never before from the days of my childhood,
  With such wild adventure on earth did I meet,
'Till your white tigers sprang at me out of the wildwood,
  And fell back exhausted in foam at my feet.


Never, O never, until I had seen thee
  Splintering the light on thy rock-shivered surge :
Had I thought how like thee with nothing between me,
  Sports my soul with its sin on Eternity's verge.


Never, O never, until I had harkened
  By night, where thy ice-crashing cataract fell,
Had I felt that I heard from the world of the darkened,
  The hoarse shout of demons flung back out of hell.


Still on me now thy smooth waters are flowing,
  Still on me now I can feel thy cold tide,
Time,—O my God! how the minutes are going,
  Beautiful serpents, how subtly ye glide.


Rapids—your restlessness ever shall haunt me,
  Till the dark, deadly current of life shall be run,
And the calm realm of Rest of heaven shall enchant me,
  Where the eagle-swan swims on the unsetting sun.

ALFRED D. WOODHULL.

# THE NATIONAL THANKSGIVING HYMN.

[*From the Hymn Book.*]

---

God of the passing year, to thee
  Our hymn of gratitude we raise;
With swelling heart and bended knee,
  We offer thee our song of praise.


We bless thy name, Almighty God,
  For all the kindness thou hast shown
To this fair land our fathers trod,
  This land we fondly call our own.


Here Freedom spreads her banner wide,
  And casts her soft and hallowed ray;
For thou our country's arms didst guide,
  And lead them on their conquering way.


We praise thee, that the Gospel light
  Through all our land its radiance sheds—
Scatters the shades of error's might,
  And heavenly blessings round us spreads.

When foes without and foes within,
With threatening ills our land have pressed,
Thou hast our nation's bulwark been,
And smiling sent us peaceful rest.

## THE BERG AND THE BARK.

The Ice King set sail from the Berserk's lone land;
His ship was an iceberg, unloos'd from the strand;
In the storm and the darkness, its cold shrouds were
    spread
On its towering masthead, so spectral and dread.

Like a chain'd fiend unbound, from the far land of Thor,
Rush'd the Wind from his caves, on that shadowy shore;
And, shrieking in fury, swept on in his might,
Attended by one—the Black Demon of Night.

With the roar of the whirlwind, the speed of the flame,
Remorseless, resistless, right onward they came;
Then, leaping the ice-crusted ship, cold and hoar,
Their shriek, wild as Nornor's, rang back o'er the shore.

As the Wind's frenzied voices swell'd out on the sky,
They parted the clouds on its track rolling by;
And soft shone the moon, with a silvery beam,
Like a smile on the face of a child in a dream.

There, there stood the Ice King, bright, baleful and cold,
And grim as the Jarls and the Vikings of old;
And hailstones, like diamonds, bejeweled his crown,
Majestic as Odin, of Norseland renown.


He spoke not, he turned not, but, pulseless and pale,
He reck'd not the billow, nor voice of the gale;
On the treacherous track, his ship knew but too well,
Like Loki, he rush'd on his errand of hell.


Not a league from the weird ship, a staunch little bark
Darted on in her course, without warning or mark;
She noted the iceberg's pale, glittering face,
And her doom, should she touch but its terrible base.


On her deck, in the dread hush of speechless despair,
Stood brave men, and children, and womanhood fair;
A shuddering horror sealed fast every lip,
As nearer they came to the merciless ship.


Unmoved, midst the storm, stood the helmsman so brave,
Little reck'd at the wind or the tempest-toss'd wave;
Beside him was Astrid, his fair, winsome child,
Looking out on the Ocean, all boist'rous and wild.

"What is that, oh, Father! What is that?" she cried,
"That moves like a ghost far out on the tide?
See, Father, it's coming,—it almost is here,—
It looks like a bright frozen cloud rolling near!"

The maiden listen'd;—mysterious and slow
Came borne on the whirlwind a voice soft and low;
In her dark, prayerful eyes lay no boding of ill,
For she heard above all that voice "small and still."

The favoring wind, now shifting its course,
'Gainst the glittering berg beat with pitiless force;
It work'd and it writh'd in its terrible might,
As the blast swept in fury its pinnacled height.

O'er the deck of the bark the storm-crested wave
Dash'd relentless. Still daring, the helmsman so brave,
By the soft, loving light of the radiant moon
Turn'd her course from the Ice King's cold ship of
    doom.

And now, as the bark o'er the wild waters sped,
From her fate by the God of the storms safely led,
There came from the iceberg a deafening roar,
That struck horror to hearts horror-stricken before.

The Ice King had vanished ;—swift, sudden, the shock
That dash'd the doom'd berg 'gainst the granite-ribb'd
    rock,
Uprearing its crest 'neath the billow; the bright
Ship struck, and from base to its towering height,


Shiv'ring and reeling, with one mighty crash,
As instant as thought or the lightning's dread flash,
It quiver'd and broke o'er the black, angry wave,
Then silently sank to its fathomless grave.

T. E. GREEN.

(Class of "1880.")

THEOLOGICAL SEMINARY.

## VIOLETS.

There's a story told
In a legend old,
Of a maiden of heavenly birth;
But a silver dart
Had pierced her heart,
And she loved a youth of earth.


So she stole away,
In the dawn of day,
From her place by the throne of Jove;
And through summer hours,
From the blooming flowers,
She blushed her heart's fond love.


But the spying eye
Of the sun on high,
P

Saw the maiden in her disguise;
   And when evening late
     Had swung the gate,
And lighted the lantered skies;


   •He told her love
     To the gods above,
And their anger grew fierce and dread;
     And their sentence dire,
     Like the Thunderer's fire,
Fell full on her drooping head.


   They bound her then
     With a golden chain,
And from heaven's arches high,
     Like a wandering star
     In the azure far,
She fell through the evening sky.


   On earth she fell,
     In a grassy dell
Where the whispering flowers grew;
     And the morning bright
     Kissed her tears to light,
'Till they blossomed in violets blue.

# HOPE ON.

Hope on! though every dream of life should perish,
    And youth's gay flush like summer flowers consume;
Though all the dearest ties you love to cherish
    Elude your grasp like shadows from the tomb.
Though friends betray, and fickle fortune slight you,
    Though every prop you lean upon is gone,
Though night shuts in without one star to light you,
    And tempests howl around you, still, hope on.

Though like a pilot on the rocks of danger
    Thy lone soul looks out from her idle helm;
Yet seems, O God, to drift in as a stranger
    Before the balmy lights in that fair realm;
Hope on! the howling blast will sink beneath you,
    And nature's storm-king leave the sea more calm.
The starless night though long, at last shall wreathe you
    With the full glory of the sunlight's palm.

What though I feel my hold on this earth weaken,
    What though death drop his mantle down apace,

My soul shall know Thee as a ship its beacon,
  And sun itself at last upon his face.
Hope on, dear heart, hope on and on forever,
  Though all thou hope for on this earth be gone ;
For I am sure that God will never, never,
  Crush the brave heart that still in Him hopes on ;
That still in Him, defiant, grand, hopes on.

# PATRIOTISM.

Point them to the summits, where the patriots bled,
To every village where lie their glorious dead ;
Point where their bosoms met the dreadful shock,
Their only corselet the rude rustic's frock :
Point where they mustered to the gathering horn,
Where titled chieftains curled their lips in scorn ;
Point where their leader bade the lines advance,
No musket wavering in the lion's glance ;
Point where they fainted in the forced retreat,
And tracked the snow-drifts with their bleeding feet;
Point where their banners tossing in the blast,
Bore ever ready faithful to the last
Through storm and battle, till they waved again,
O'er Yorktown's hills, and Saratoga's plain.

## RICHARD ARNOLD GREENE.

(Class of "1878.")

# PRIDE AND HUMILITY.

———

Treading 'neath those oaks tremendous,
  I was bound by Wonder's spell:
Dark they rose in height stupendous,
  Murmuring loud with ceaseless swell:
"Wind or blast can never rend us."


While I watched them, all alluring,
  Scorners of the scathing storm,
Still again they 'spoke, assuring
  That in grand and massive form
They would ever stand enduring.


Now, in hidden beauty lying,
  Each one drooping low its head,
'Neath those ancient oaks undying,
  From their mossy, humble bed,
I could hear the violets sighing:

" Ye who with unquenched ambition
  Watch us from your lofty height,
Spurn our dark, unfamed position
  Oaks majestic, in your sight
Ever low is our condition."


Time unhindered, swiftly gliding
  With his mighty hand works change ;
E'en those oaks, so strong abiding,
  Lay in his extended range,
In their ageless power confiding.


Lo ! He's torn them far asunder,
  While his aid, the exultant Wind,
Claims them for his own rich plunder.
  Still, in lowly grace I find
Living violets, and I wonder—


If this may not be a warning,
  Telling us how vain is Pride ;
That Humility adorning,
  Borne along Time's raging tide,
Shall outlast the blasts of scorning,
  And with olden charm abide
Till the fair eternal morning.

# NO, NO, IT IS NOT DYING.

No, no, it is not dying,
　To go unto our God—
This gloomy earth forsaking,
Our journey homeward taking,
　Along the starry road.


No, no, it is not dying,
　Heaven's citizen to be—
A wreath immortal wearing,
And rest unbroken sharing,
　From care and conflict free.


No, no, it is not dying,
　To wear a lordly crown—
Among God's people dwelling,
The glorious triumph swelling,
　Of Him whose sway we own.

# E. SPENCER MILLER.

(CLASS OF "1836.")

[*Author of "Caprices."*]

## IGDRASIL.

For the Present holds in it the whole Past and the whole Future, as the Life tree—Igdrasil—wide-waving, many-toned, has its roots down deep in the Death kingdoms, among the oldest dead dust of men, and with its boughs reaches always beyond the stars, and in all times and places is one and the same life tree.—CARLYLE.


Igdrasil—weird and sombre tree,—
My spirit's awe goes up to thee,
And shadows chill my revery.


I lie beneath thee, in a night
Of phantom-shapes and fitful light,
And fancy shudders in her flight.


The voices of the countless dead,
The echoes of the ages fled,
All times are murmuring in thy shade.

And, deeper as the darkness lowers,
I feel the presence of the hours,—
The silent fates of human powers.


Remorseless hours, that on thy bough
Are brooding in an endless now,
Upon the steadfast change below;


While o'er me the breath of doom,
In fitful gusts from out the gloom,
Is blowing into years to come—


Igdrasil—weird and sombre tree—
My spirit kneeleth unto thee,
And wrestles with thy mystery.


The green above me flourisheth;
Thy roots are in the grave beneath;
I know that life is fed by death;


I know that what is quick to-day,
Is born of being past away—
A new conception of decay.

The ceaseless generations tell
That life and death are seething well
In Time, the chemist's aludel.


For even as I muse around,
A leaf is falling to the ground,
But lo! the night gives up no sound.


But still its fellows whisper there,
And shiver in the pregnant air,
And legion are the shapes they wear.


And legion are the tones that rise
In mimicry of strifes and sighs,
The burdens of all histories.


Igdrasil,—weird and sombre tree,—
My spirit goeth forth to thee,
And yearneth to her destiny.


And as the twilight of the Past
Comes up thro' that perspective east,
I see a trembling shadow cast.

A shadow without line or mark,
And restless as the wrecking bark—
A shadow trembling on the dark.


A shadow on whose surface swim,
In phantom pictures vague and dim,
The fragments of all life and time.


And yet the shadow of a tree,
Whose trunk and branches sway with thee,
But lengthen to infinity.


A tree where slow mine eye receives
A vision of thy boughs and leaves
That shiver as the shadow heaves.


The spell is o'er; the doubtful light
Has faded from my aching sight,
Yet still thy voice is on the night.


Igdrasil—weird and sombre tree—
The Past and Present merge in thee;
The Present is alone with me.

# THE DYING SKEPTIC.

Peace, coward heart ;
Stand fast and fear not as the hollow night
Deepens about thee, and the muffled step
Of the invisible, chill messenger
Draws near and nearer on the echoless hours.
Thou, who hast questioned dim astrologies,
Why start and shudder at a new conjunction
In the uncertain, shifting horoscope ?
Thou, who alone in truant haunts of thought
Has loved the thinnest outside air of truth,
Where reason grapples languidly with doubt,
The actual wrestles with the Infinite ;—
Why clutch and grasp for some material hold,
When the whole girding atmosphere of life
Sinks from about thee, and thou art in space ?
Thou who hast left thy one own beautiful sun,
The fireside of a planetary household,
And, in the dream of fancy's marvellous sleep
Worshipped the innumerable hosts of heaven,
That, in the orderings of Divinity,
Appear but in the night, and then far off.

And but to him that waking, against Nature
From out the broken rest of care or crime,
Seeth above him, in that solemn hour,
Signs supernatural, paths of meteors :
Why dost thou falter when thou may'st be free,
And roam God's boundless government a child,
Not of the earth, but of the universe ?          •
Thou who hast struggled with thy destiny,
And, in the fever of thine inner vision,
Hast curst this passive chrysalis of thine,
Why stand all palsied when the unseen hand
Opens Time's outward gate, and leaves thee nude
In the full presence of Eternity ?

MALCOLM MACDONALD.

(Class of " 1861.")

# EXCERPTS FROM "GUATEMOZIN."

Ah! I will strike
With mailed hand on Fame, till every bolt ․
And hinge shall shake within their portal-seat;
As he who laid his sword within the warp
Of Destiny, and held it woven there ;
Eternal as Orion's starry blade,
Which out no arm may draw, or it will cut
A gap in Nature, high heaven's law be broke,
And chaos rule the darkened void again.


Am I a brute, to crop the herbage of content in
    times like these ?


I'll practice on his vents of whims and humours.
Till, like a windy flute, he pipes my way.

Kiss her on the lips; sweet Acalan is mine,
For I shall send so fair a shaft, thy body
Will open lips, and kiss thy life away.


That strange, uncounted sense—instinctive fear—
Sniffed, like a deer that scents the tainted air,
The coming evil.


Strike at their faces—there all the senses come
To learn of you, and let the lesson be
Blind eyes, deaf ears, dumb mouths—
Death—Death.


I felt a sudden quickening of air, as if a god had
turned and looked on me.


Ah! what are we?  We crumble in the hand,
As butterflies leave on our fingers dust,
Go lame, and die, killed by the slightest touch.


I saw our forces last, a narrow ribbon, that fluttered in a wind of men.

He is of perfect force—a fortress of expedients;
I marvel at him—no misfortune daunts,
But strengthens more to counterplot with fate.


Delay confesses weakness, 'tis the pause
For breath that comes between the lifted sword
Of weary fighter, and his trembling stroke,
What time the warrior takes to run him through.


O Love, thou juggler of the heart!


First I will ply my arguments to blow
Red hot his temper, then I'll call my hammers, and
we will forge him to our purpose tight.


What? Hath my reason gone, my ears turned liars,
my eyes deceived, and my memory broken,
that its fragments patch so wrongly?


Such victories surely defeat themselves.


This open garden—this all-seeing sun—are gossips.

Q

HENRY CLOW.

Author of a volume of unpublished poems.

## OSSIAN.

Oh! for a spark of Ossian's native fire,
To wake my song, and touch my silent lyre!
On wildest wing my muse would speed her way
To "Selma's Hall," where midnight visions play!
Where Fancy pictures, midst the stately trees,
The ghost of Ossian, beckoning on the breeze.

# LINES ON LEAVING HOME.

Farewell, farewell! my native shore!
Dear, happy scenes, a long adieu!
O fond remembrance! yet once more
Methinks I take the parting view!

As some sweet flower in fragrance borne,
Beyond the sea when it is dead;
E'en so at midnight and at morn,
Still shine visions that are fled.

Oft have I strayed near Allen's stream,
When light of evening on it lay!
How pleasant soon 'twill be to dream
Of scenes like thine, tho' far away :

The rustic cot; the village green;
The winding stream that smooths along
The hawthorn shade, where lovers stray
To shun the watchful noontide throng!

Come, fancy, with thy airy wing!
  O! come with all thy cloudy train!
'Tis Nature calls!   Haste, phantom, bring
  These balmy scenes to me again.


She comes!· Methink I mark the rill
  Where lilies kiss the crystal stream!
She comes!—submissive to her will
  I haste to drink the passing dream.

ELBERT S. PORTER.

THEOLOGICAL SEMINARY.

## A THRENODY.

— —— —

A Smile!   A Tear!
A Hope!   A Fear!
Like ripples on the stream,
Like moonlight's fading beam,
   They come—they pass.
   Ah me, alas!
This life is vapor—
A flickering taper!
In flowing sympathies, in surging sorrows,
In hopeful ecstacies, in glad to-morrows,
Its rapid current runs its mystic race,
And man at last awakes in Death's embrace.


A Truth!   A Lie!
A Joy!   A Sigh!
Flow mingled in a wave
That swallows, as the grave,

Both good and ill !
Mysterious still
Its surface shining,
Its depths repining !
With warring passions that can never rest,
The heart is throbbing in the troubled breast ;
Eager for joy, it seizes present pain,
And worships phantom pleasures o'er again.


A Birth !   A Breath !
A Toll !   A Death !
Then yawns the hungry tomb
To which all flesh must come,—
And life is done,
The goal is won !
Dreams all are ended,
Strength all expended.
In awful silence now the dust asleep
Throbs with no love, nor hears if friendship weep ;
The marble cold, the flower-encircled knoll,
Conceal and guard the palace of a soul.


A Soul !   A Sin !
Ah, how !   Ah, when
Shall these disparted be ?
What holy ministry

Shall work the cure,
And make Faith sure
That piteous Heaven
Death's hold hath riven?
A loving Presence shines upon our sight—
Incarnate Truth diffusing living light!

# HESPERION.

The day's great portals slowly close,
   Swung by the fairy-fingered hours,
And evening's colors, flaked with rose,
   Wave from the caps of cloudy towers.


The wreathing winds are hushed to rest,
   Pillowed in snowy cloud-fleece fair;
Dark night has bared her ebon breast,
   And set her jewels in her hair.


The soft, low-beaming star of even
   Woos with a kiss the flying day,
Till the far-reaching blue of heaven
   Blushes beneath its mantle gray.


The moon, pale abbess of the sky,
   Peers from her cloudy cloister bars,
And kneels neath heaven's arches high,
   Counting her rosary of stars.

# SUMMER TIME.

All the day
Bees are humming in the clover ;
Flowers gay,
Blooming all the wide fields over ;


Summer sky,
Laughing at the babbling river
Grain-fields high,
With the truant breezes quiver ;


Early moon,
Rising in the blushing even ;
Taper stars,
In the altar arch of heaven ;


Kisses sweet,
Stolen from the willing maiden ;
Whispered vows,
With life's early fragrance laden ;

Lazily
Bees are humming in the clover;
Well-a-day,
Summer time will soon be over.

# A YEAR AGO.

A year ago,
Beyond the meadow's ruined stile,
 We gathered flowers
 Through summer hours ;
I loved you dearly for the while,
 A year ago.


A year ago
Your love was like the violets true ;
 But winter white
 Hath brought its blight ;
Your heart is not the heart I knew
 A year ago.

[*Authoress.*]

# A THRUSH'S SONG.

Underneath a leafy cover,
  Green with morning-wealth of June,
Wanting still, like gift of lover,
  Craving even greater boon,
Deeper chords of light to perfect summer's fullness,
  love's high noon;

Just apart from all the glitter
  Of a busy crystal world,
Where, amid quick human twitter,
Leaping shuttle wrought bright fancies, girded wheels
  obedient whirled;

Just a little from the glimmer,
  From the footfalls' tuneless tread,
With the distance ever dimmer,
  Rose, so calm o'ershadowed,
Sound of lusty drum and hautboy, with clear flute voice
  interlaid.

Notes exultant, loud outpouring,
　　Chant of nations, lightly bound
With frail melody, uproaring
　　On the people, gathered round,
Resting from the glare a little, from the wearing light
　　and sound.

Ears of loyal Britons tingling,
　　Hark'ning there, " God save the Queen ;"
Erin's children's tears commingling
　　At " The Wearing of the Green,"
Thinking of a loveless bondage, truer trust that might
　　have been.

Sounds of wrathful people seeming
　　Storming through the " Marseillaise,"
Stirred a land, nigh dead in dreaming,
　　Through Hortense's song of praise,
Through its wailing sadness tolling bells of old chival-
　　ric days.

Through sad France's slumber breaking
　　Germany's triumphant hymn,
Amid people's, eager waking,
　　Watching Rhine-lights growing dim,
Hearing clear a weary nation struggling sore with
　　spectres grim.

In the nations' anthems swelling,
   Ever twanged some chord of wrong;
Broken notes in anguish welling,
   Even in our starlit song—
Shadowy notes from swamp and prairie mingling with
   the suffering throng.

Stilled at last the music's clamour,
   Drum and hautboy laid to rest,
Softly through the silence' glamour
   Stole the light wind of the west,
Gently parted the green branches, tenderly each leaf
   caressed.

And a sudden thrill of sweetness,
   Mellow, careless, glad and clear,
Love's noon-song in its completeness,
   Poured in peaceful nature's ear,
From a thrush's throat of silver—happy song without
   one tear

Fell like precious, heav'n-dropped token
   'Mid the elements of strife,
'Mid the melodies, grief-broken,
   Blare of trumpet, shriek of fife
Only with undarkened blessings was the thrush's sing-
   ing rife.

Where the ways were broad and ordered
England's Indian blossoms flamed ;
Here, where guarding thickets bordered,
Bloom of May June's sunshine claimed,
Lifting, 'mid the throngs of people, glance, half-fearing,
half-ashamed;

Trembling at the cymbals crashing
Through the ancient solitude,
Till the thrush's sweetness flashing,
With its wild-wood joy imbued,
Seemed a covenant from heaven, arc of promise, rain-
bow-hued.

In the upper silence singing,
Hidden minstrel, unafraid,
In the sunlit branches, swinging,
By the west wind, whispering, swayed,
All the lower tumult silenced in the clear, blue depths
o'erhead ;

Whence the peace of heaven, descending,
Filled the bird's song, true and clear,
Lightsome duty sweetness lending,
Joy o'erbrimming in its cheer,
Freedom on his pinions resting, sunshine soft, and
heaven near.

Careless strength and free heart blending
   In each note's melodious mirth,
   Calm within a pure soul bending,
   Praising for its heavenly birth,
For its gift of soaring pinions, lightening so the bonds
   of earth.

   With that clear and sudden sweetness
   Sober fancies swept along,
   And its wild-wood, perfect muteness
   Seemed our country's truer song,
Sunshine soft, and heaven near it, and no undertone of
   wrong.

   So, methought, her clear voice ringing,
   Should in strength of freedom rise,
   With the sweetness of its singing,
   Every evil exorcise;
Blessing for her children winning through her nearness
   to the skies.

PHILIP FRENEAU.

(Class of " 1771.")

# THE INDIAN.

Author of several volumes of Poems.

[*From Griswold's American Poets.*]

In spite of all the learned have said,
   I still my old opinion keep ;
The posture that we give the dead
   Points out the soul's eternal sleep.


Not so the ancients of these lands,
   The Indian, when from life released
Again is seated with his friends,
   And shares again the joyous feast.


His imaged birds, and painted bowl,
   And ven'son for a journey dressed,
Bespeak the nature of the soul,
   Activity that knows no rest.

R

By midnight moons o'er moistening dews,
  In vestments for the chase arrayed,
The hunter still the deer pursues,
  The hunter and the deer—a shade.

# PSALM XC.

Author of metrical version of the Psalms, some of which have been adopted into our Hymnology.

**1.**

Lord! in all generations Thou
Our dwelling-place hast been;
Before the mountains were brought forth,
Before the world was seen:

**2.**

Or ever Thou hadst formed the earth,
Or spread the heavens abroad,
From everlasting, Lord, Thou art
To everlasting, God.

**3.**

Back to destruction and to dust,
Thou turnest man again;
To all our mortal race Thou say'st,
" Return, ye sons of men."

4.

A thousand years—to us so vast—
O Lord! are in Thy sight
As yesterday when it is past,
And as a watch of night.

5.

As with a sweeping flood, our race
Thou carriest away;
They are asleep, yea, like the grass
That grows at morn are they.

6.

At morn it groweth up and blooms,
At eve cut down, doth fade;
O Lord! Thine anger us consumes,
Thy wrath makes us afraid.

7.

All our iniquity and sin
Before Thee Thou dost place;
Our secret sins thou settest in
The brightness of Thy face.

### 8.

In Thy consuming wrath, behold
Our days waste to their end ;
And as a tale that has been told,
So all our years we spend.

### 9.

The days of all the years we see,
Are three-score years and ten ;
And if by strength they four-score be,
Their strength itself is vain.

### 10.

For it in labor is employed,
And sorrow every day,
'Tis soon cut off, we are destroyed,
And swiftly fly away.

### 11.

Who of Thine anger knows the power?
Who can endure Thy rod ?
According even to Thy fear,
So is Thy wrath, O God.

### 12.

Teach us—since death is ever nigh—
To number all our days,
That we may earnestly apply
Our hearts to wisdom's ways.

CHARLES W. SHIELDS.

(Class of "1844.")

## THE TRIUMPH OF LIBERTY.

O Liberty! again thy story,
    Which oft before thy sons have told,
The rolling cycles swell with glory,
    The story that can ne'er grow old:
How Truth and Right have battl'd Error,
    How patriots rush'd to martyrs' graves,
    How freemen scorn'd the chains of slaves,
And tyrants fell with rage and terror.
            Rejoice, O Liberty!
            Take courage from the past:
        Press on! press on! till victory
        Shall crown thy brows at last.


Lo! on these western waters drifted,
    In flying bands across the main,
A chosen race of heroes sifted,
    As from the chaff is thresh'd the grain:
They come, the van of eastern sages;

They bear the richest spoils of Time,
And hail the new, imperial clime
Adorn'd of old for riper ages.
    Rejoice, O Liberty!


Hark! hark! what groans and shouts are blend-
    ing!
New England calls with struggling breath!
Virginia's tongue of flame is sending
    The cry of "Liberty or Death!"
While Jersey sees the war-clouds lower,
    Her face by hireling legions marr'd,
    Her dauntless brow with battles scarr'd,
Till victory gleams on Nassau's tower.
    Rejoice, O Liberty!


Ah! bitter, bitter and defiant
    The surges of the civic strife,
Ere like a full-arm'd infant giant,
    The nation struggled into life!
And long, O long shall be recited,
    What glories shroud the fallen brave,
    How virtue blossoms from their grave,
In arts increased and states united.
    Rejoice, O Liberty!

Nor yet, O Liberty, is ended
  Thy march of glorious agony ;
Not till all tongues and peoples blended
  At length acclaim, The world is free !
Not till one nation to another
  Around the globe shall roll the strain,
  The West rejoin the East again,
And man hail every man his brother.
    Rejoice, O Liberty !


O Liberty ! then be thy story
  Still, still with quenchless fervor told
As rolling cycles swell its glory ;
  The story that can ne'er grow old,
While yet the radiant face of Nature
  Is darken'd by a single slave,
  As long as Virtue claims the brave,
And man hath faith in his Creator.
    Rejoice, O Liberty !
      Take courage from the past ;
    Press on ! press on ! till victory
      Shall crown thy brows at last !

## THE NATION'S HOPE.

O second Land of Promise,
  E'en of this latter day,
A promise that in mercies
  God's finger did portray.


Land in whose wondrous progress
  Was His right arm revealed,
Who did her hosts encompass
  " With favor as a shield."


Land of God's preparation,
  As centuries rolled on ;
Scene of his great salvation,
  For centuries to come.


Land thence, of God's adoption
  Where he designs to raise
Through many generations,
  A Temple to his praise.

Land of the pilgrim exiled,
Land of the would-be-free,
Land of the open Bible,
Thence land of liberty.


Land of God's benediction
In all that makes us great,
Where duty joined to privilege,
In union stand complete.


The light of her example
Has flashed across the sea:
Just where the burdened nations
Are struggling to be free.


And they, in that rejoicing,
E'en now begin to raise
For disenthralled religion
The voice of prayer and praise.


To take complete possession
Of this inheritance,
Behold, in long succession,
A peaceful host advance.

To plant the rose of Sharon
　Through all the prairies wild
The lesson of the lilies,
　Tell to each saddened child.


And Gilead's balm to carry
　Unto each nook and glen—
Commission sanitary,
　Commission Christian then.


And where the miner's treasure
　Is hailed with gladdened eyes,
The priceless pearl to proffer,
　But proffer without price.


Till on the Nation's Highway
　God's temples mark the road,
And from each mountain by-way
　Sounds household praise to God.


Till from the stormy ocean
　That bounds us on the east,
Unto that World of waters
　That terminates the west.

And from the Central Valley,
    And o'er our broad domain,
Each generation passing,
    Shall to the next proclaim


The wonders, of his dealing,
    Who did our fathers lead ;
His grace for grace revealing,
    In every time of need.


His mighty acts tell over,
    And ne'er His love forget,
Who in His mercy saved us,
    For sacred union yet.

# HUMOROUS POETRY.

# DIE SCHOENE WITTWE.

### THE POOTY VIDDER.

[*From the Hans Breitman's Ballads.*]

Dat pooty liddle vidder
Vot we doshn't vish to name,
Ish still leben on dat liddle shtreet,
A-doin shuss de same.
De glerks aroundt de gorners
Somedimes goes round to zee
How de tarlin liddle vitchy ees,
Und ask er how she pe.
Dey lofes her ver' goot liquoer,
Dey loves her liddle shtore;
Dey loves her liddle paby,
But dey lofes die vidder more.
To talk mih dat shveet vidder,
Ven she hands das lager round,
Vill make der shap dat does id
Pe happy, ve'll be pound.

S

Dat ish if ve can vell pelieve
De glerks vat drinks das peer,
Who goes in dere for nodings elshe,
Put simply for to zee her.

# O, "MEIN FRACK IST IM PFAND-HAUS."

Mine tress-goat is shpouted, mine tress-goat aint here,
While you in your ball robes go splurgin, mein tear!
To barties mit you I'm infited you know,
Boot my pest coat ish shpouted—mine poots are no go.
To hell mit mine Onkel—dat rasgally knave!
Dis pledgin und pawnin has mate me his slafe.
Ven I dink of his sign-bost, den dree dimes I bawl,
While mine black pants hang lonely und dark on de
    wall.


Goot night to dees fine lofe, so lofely und rich,
Mein tress-goat is shpouted, gonfount efery stitch!
I dinks dat old Satan troo all mine affairs,
Lofe, business, und fun, has been sewin his tares,
My tress-goat ish shpouted—mine tress-goat aint here,
While you in your glorie go shinin, mein tear;
Und de luck of der teufel ish loose ofer all,
While mine black pants hang lonely und dark on de
    wall.

# HANS BREITMAN'S IDEA OF "BOLITICS."

Dese ish de brincibles I holts,
  Und dose in vitch I run:
Dey ish fixed firm and immutaple
  Ash te course of de ternal sun;
Boot if you ton't abbrove of dem—
  Blease nodice vot I say,
I shall only pe too happy
  To alter them right afay.

# PLAIN LANGUAGE FROM THE IRRECON-
## CILABLES, CONCERNING A RECENT
### UNPLEASANTNESS.

Which we wish to remark,
 And our language is squa-ah,
That a man which is dark,
 And has kinks in his hai-ah,
Isn't coming to lectures with " we uns,"
 And " we uns " consent to be thea-ah.


Which the lecture was that
 On the "Science of Mind,"
And our hearts as we sat
 Were at peace with mankind,
When who should come in but a nigg-ah
 And squat on a seat just behind.


We looked up at Mac,
 And he rose with a sigh,
And remarked—its a fac'—
 Well, I wish I may die

If I'm going to sit here with a nigg-ah,
And we left without any reply.


We repeat the remark,
  And our language is squa-ah,
That a man which is dark,
  And has kinks in his hai-ah,
Isn't coming to College with " we uns,"
  And " we uns " consent to be thea-ah.

# WHAT SHE SAID ON THE WAY HOME.

### AFTER THE POPULAR SCIENCE LECTURE.

Yes, I think it was perfectly splendid—
I'm sure I feel awfully wise,
With my head full of glaciers and icebergs,
Of such a ridiculous size;
And the masses of what do you call it—
The dirt that is ever so old—
And came down on the ice to New Jersey,
It must have been horribly cold.

The views, too, were perfectly lovely?
Especially Mont Blanc and the Alps;
Though the last ones were perfectly frightful—
Those men with the clubs and the scalps.
Well, maybe they didn't have scalps—
They frightened me all the same,
And that animal—wasn't he horrid.
The—what–did–he–say–was–his–name?

O! I perfectly dote upon science:
  I think it's just jolly good fun:
And I wish I were going on your expe-
  Dition, with knapsack and gun.
Mamma says I'm growing strong-minded,
  And should cut off my hair, and all that,
Though eye-glasses would not become me,
  And how could I keep on my hat?


Here's the end of our walk—Good night!
  You may call Wednesday evening, Rob,
And we'll talk of the Glacial Epoch,
  And the wonderful thingumabob.

## VARIATIONS ON THE C STRING.

Old Mundus shudders in his ribs
And ponders in his mists,
When millionaires with patent nibs
Prepare financial lists.


For he has felt the cable thrown
Around his mighty ribs,
And dreads the sharp, magnetic tone
Of these commercial nibs.


The Psalmist, in his wisdom, said,
"Deep calleth unto deep."
Three thousand years hath he been dead;
How green his sayings keep.

And modern genius idly sings
Of " music of the spheres."
Little imagining what strings
Are twisting with the years.


The daring mariner long erst
Plumbed ocean's treacherous bed ;
Lo, here the soundings lie immersed,
Conversing with the lead.*


Thus science brings the teeming womb
Of Nature to the birth,
And crowns with intellectual bloom
Her princes in the earth.

---

* Type.

# THE RECONSTRUCTION OF SOCIETY.

Air.—"*The University of Göttingen.*"

When others, once as poor as I,
Are growing rich, because they try,
While my capacity and will
Give me a taste for sitting still;
When all around me are at work,
While I prefer to act the Turk,
Or spend in drinking or at play
The greater part of every day;
And, as the upshot of it, feel
That I must either starve or steal;
The only remedy I see,
For such abuses, is the re-
Construction of society,
    Construction of society.


When others know what I know not,
Or bear in mind what I forgot
An age ago, and dare to speak

In praise of Latin and of Greek,
As if a tongue unknown to me
Of any earthly use could be ;
When bookworms are allowed to rule
In University and School,
While I, because I am a fool,
Or, happen, by the merest chance,
To have learned nothing save to dance,
Am set aside, or thrust away,
Or not allowed to have my say ;
The only remedy I see
For such abuses, is the re-
Construction of society,
    Construction of society.


When judges frown and parsons scold,
Because a gentleman makes bold
To laugh at superstitious saws,
And violate oppressive laws ;
When pinching want will not atone
For taking what is not your own ;
When public sentiment proscribes
The taking of judicial bribes,
And with indignant scorn regards
The gentleman who cheats at cards ;

When men of wit no longer dare
To tell a lie, or even swear;
The only remedy I see
For such abuses, is the re-
Construction of society,
    Construction of society.


When, after turning round and round,
And occupying every ground:
As preacher, poet, rhetorician,
Philanthropist and politician,
Ascetic, saint, and devotee,
Neologist and pharisee,
I seek in vain to gain respect
By founding a new-fangled sect,
And find the world so cautious grown
That I must be the sect alone;
The only remedy I see
For such abuses, is the re-
Construction of society,
    Construction of society.


When, over and above the scorn
Of men, which leaves me thus forlorn,
I find an enemy within

Who dares to talk to me of sin,
And whispers, even in my dreams,
That my disorganizing schemes
Can never conjure black to white,
Or clearly prove that wrong is right,
A nuisance that can never cease
Till conscience learns to hold its peace,
And men no longer can be awed
By apprehensions of a God—
Ah! these are griefs for which I see
No solace even in the re-
Construction of society,
  Construction of society.

# TO THE SPIRIT OF DREAMS.

How evanescent and marine
Are thy chaotic uplands seen,
    O ever sub-lapsarian moon.
A thousand caravans of light
Were not so spherically bright,
    Nor ventilated half so soon.


Methought I stood upon a cone
Of solid allopathic stone,
    And gazed athwart the breezy skies;
When lo! from yonder hemisphere,
A vapid atrabillious tear
    Was shed by pantomimic eyes.


Adieu, Miasma, cries a voice,
In which Aleppo might rejoice,
    So peri-focal were its tones.
Adieu, Miasma, think of me
Beyond the Antinomian sea
    That covers my pellucid bones.

Again—again my bark is tossed
Upon the raging holycaust
    Of that acidulated sea :•
And diapasons pouring down
With lunar caustic join to drown,
    My transcendental epopce.

FITZ HUGH LUDLOW.

## TO A RED-HEADED GIRL.

All thy curls are winding stairs,
Where my passion nobly dares,
To mount higher, still and higher,
Though the staircase be on fire.

T

# THE JOLLY FELLOW.

### I.

There was a jolly fellow, who lived about the town,
He disapproved of toddy, and so—he *put it down;*
He attended public dinners for fun and freedom's sake,
And, like a second polycarp, went smiling to the *steak.*

### II.

His vests were irreproachable, his trowsers of the kind
Adown whose steep declivities hound rushes after hind;
They were a speaking pattern, all the tailors would agree,
But, O, alas! they were too *tight* to speak coherently.

### III.

Up half a dozen pair of stairs our hero went to bed,
With nothing but the angels and the rafters o'er his head;
And so, although he loved to be where brandy vapor
    curled,
There never was a man who lived so much above the
    world.

## IV.

No boards of all the roof were known a meeting e'er to
    hold,
And so the room was nothing but a trap for catching cold ;
There was a door—the carpenter had left the lock be_
    hind ;
It must have slipt him, as he had no " Locke upon the
    Mind."

## V.

Well plastered were the rooms below, though that's an-
    other *story*,
But now our hero's fate was *sealed* and not his *dormitory* ;
When midnight played upon his bones, airs far from
    operatic,
What wonder that an attic room should make a man
    rheumattic.

## VI.

No dome was there, no window stained with Peter and
    the keys,
But every winter brought a vast redundancy of *freeze ;*
Each empty sash groaned dolefully, as if it felt the *pain,* .
By some unearthly grammarye a-coming back again.

## VII.

Our hero's uncle used to dye, to keep himself alive,
His shop was down in Nassau street, at No. 45 ;
But when, as every *dier* must, he found his colors fail,
Before he kicked the bucket, he turned a *little pale.*

.

## VIII.

His dandy friends grew fewer, and, alas ! he found between
Their *leaving* and their *falling off,* no summer inter-
vene ;
His heart was broken, and at last this fanciest of blades,
Who used to flare in scarlet vests, preferred the *darker
shades.*

## IX.

One morning from a frowning cliff he jumped into the
sea,
Crying, "Oh ! thou mighty dying vat, behold I come
to thee ; "
You think him green, and as to that I really cannot tell,
But if he is, it is the kind they call invisible.

## X.

But, oh ! how vain to try to change the color of his days,

For he could not conceal himself behind his screen of
  *bays;*

No yarn, of all that he might spin, could hide his
  uncle's line,

For that worthy was not one of those who dye and give
  no sign.

# ERRATA.

## TABLE OF CONTENTS.

Page X, line 22, Our Dead *belongs to second line below, as anonymous*.
Page X, line 23, for 133 read 131.
Page XI, line 17, for *Alamby* read *Alamby M.*
Page XIII, line 22, for *D. M.* read *J. D. M.*

## POEMS.

Page 1, line 2, fill blank with 1845.
Page 29, line 8, for *with* read *ah!*
Page 29, line 9, for *thee* read *thou.*
Page 31, line 1, prefix *anonymous.*
Page 31, line 17, for *silenceniatus* read *silence.*
Page 34, line 1, for *palid* read *pallid.*
Page 75, line 1, for *Phillip* read *Philip.*
Page 82, line 2, for *Coblentry* read *Coblentz.*
Page 108, line 1, for *Breckenridge* read *Breckinridge.*
Page 123, line 6, for *he* read *be.*
Page 131, line 1, prefix *anonymous.*
Page 159, line 1, for *Pearson* read *Pierson.*
Page 172, line 1, for *Alamby* read *Alamby M.*
Page 216, line 2, for *now* read *nor.*
Page 219, line 1, for *Alfred D.* read *Alfred A.*
Page 243, line 9, after *shine* supply *the.*
Page 281, line 1, for *D. M.* read *J. D. M.*

www.ingramcontent.com/pod-product-compliance
Lightning Source LLC
Chambersburg PA
CBHW031404270326
41929CB00010BA/1321